Color With Your Besties
Sherri Baldy
Coloring Books

About The Artist

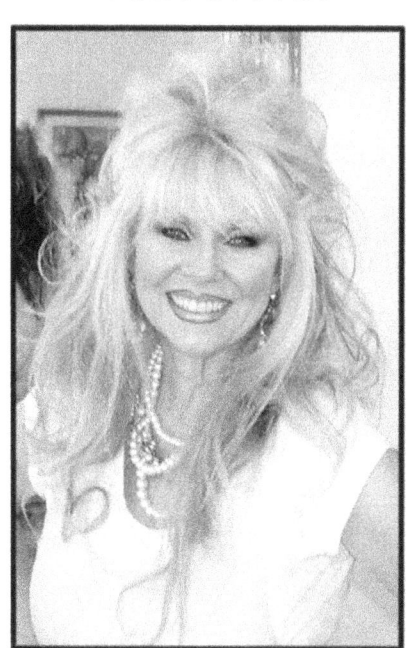

Sherri Baldy is known for her trademark Big Eyed art for over 20 plus years around the world. She is a multi media artist that is licensed on a wide range of products. Sherri lives in Riverside, Calif. with her husband on their farm (Urban Farm Diva Farms) She has two sons Kyler & Josh & two daughter Courtney & Brittany.

When she is not painting, drawing and creating craft products for the craft industry, she spends her time in the gardens at the farm and in her "Barn Studio" that is open to the public by appointment.
Sherri Baldy is now offering her Big Eyed My-Bestie artwork in coloring books.
These fun coloring books come with 2 copies of each image for you to color, or better yet, have a Bestie party and color with one of your Besties Pals or keep them all to yourself :-)
Most of all have FUN, Color, Relax and Enjoy!

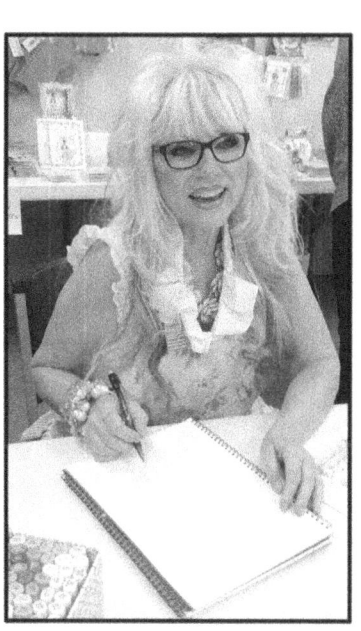

www.MyBestiesShop.com
Sherri Baldy My Besties Coloring Books in Riverside CA.
Copyright Sherri Baldy ~ My-Besties TM

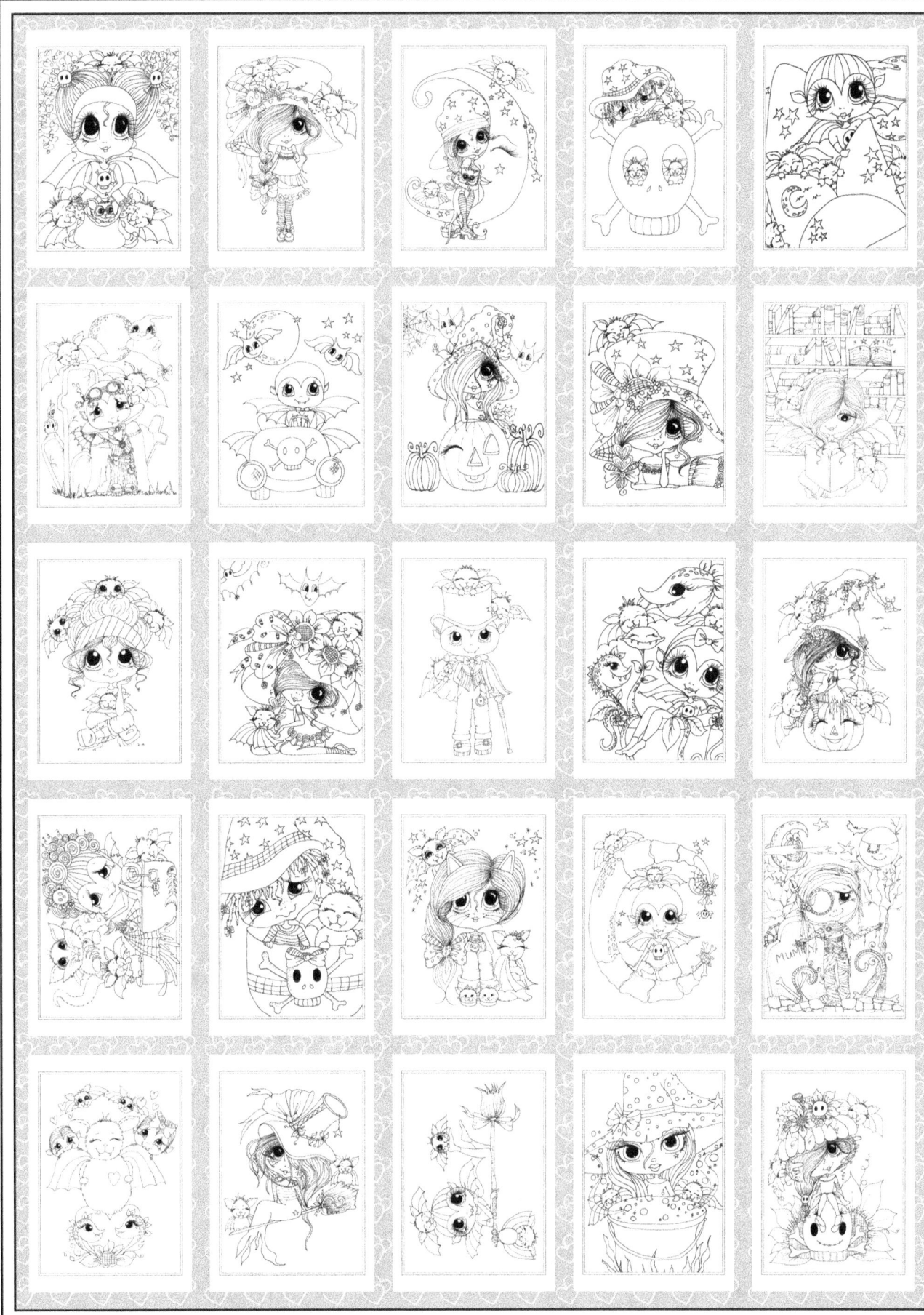

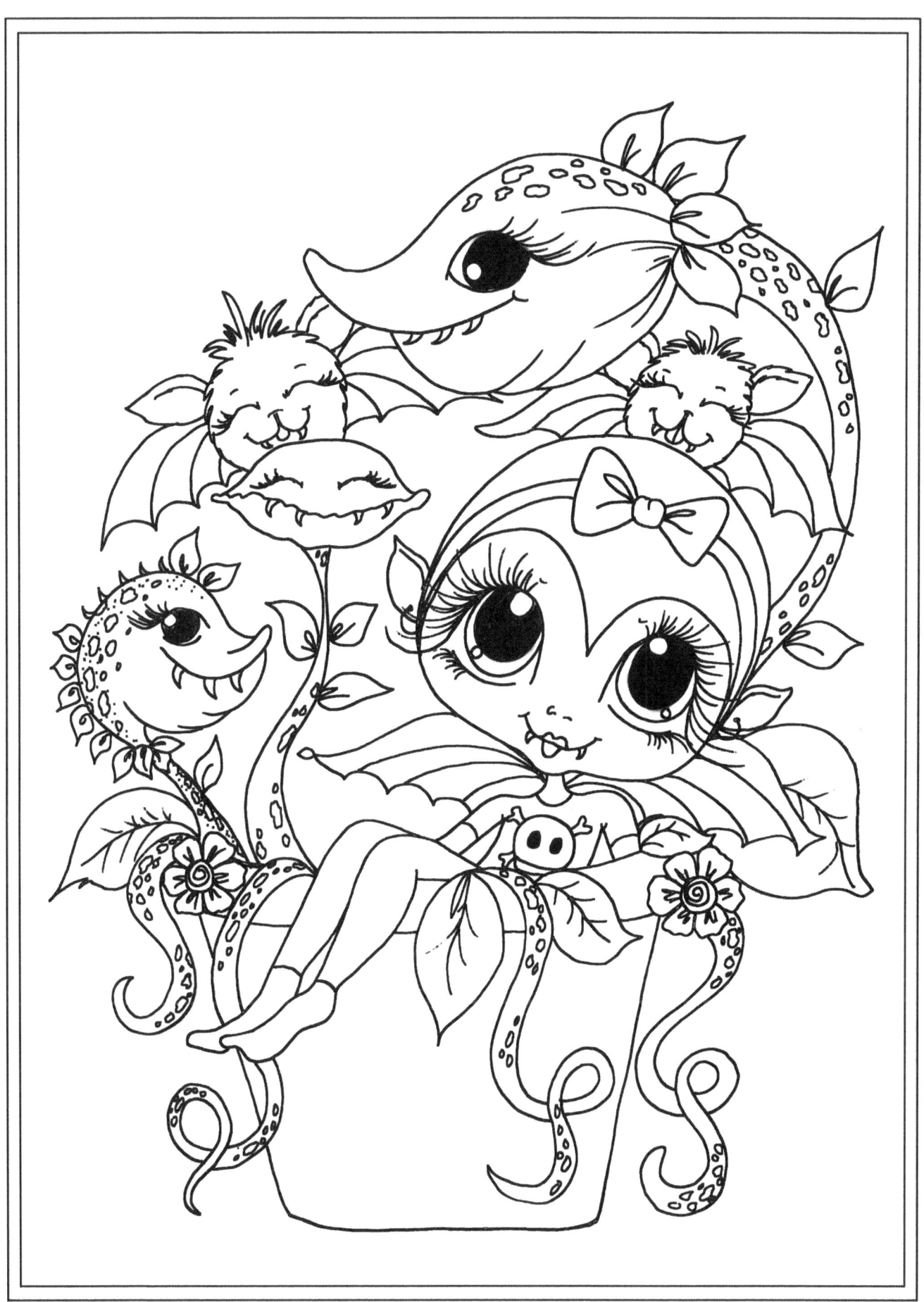

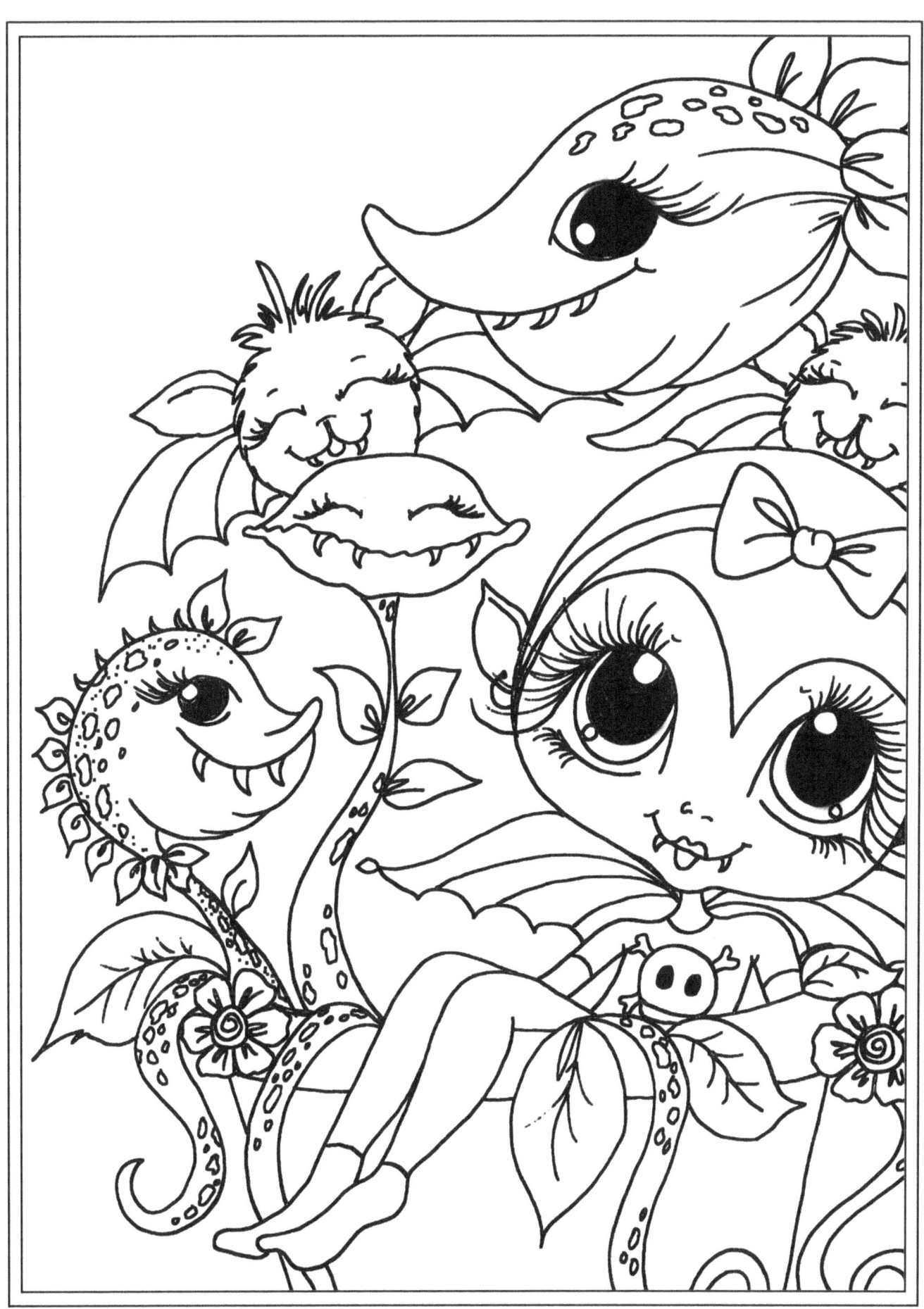

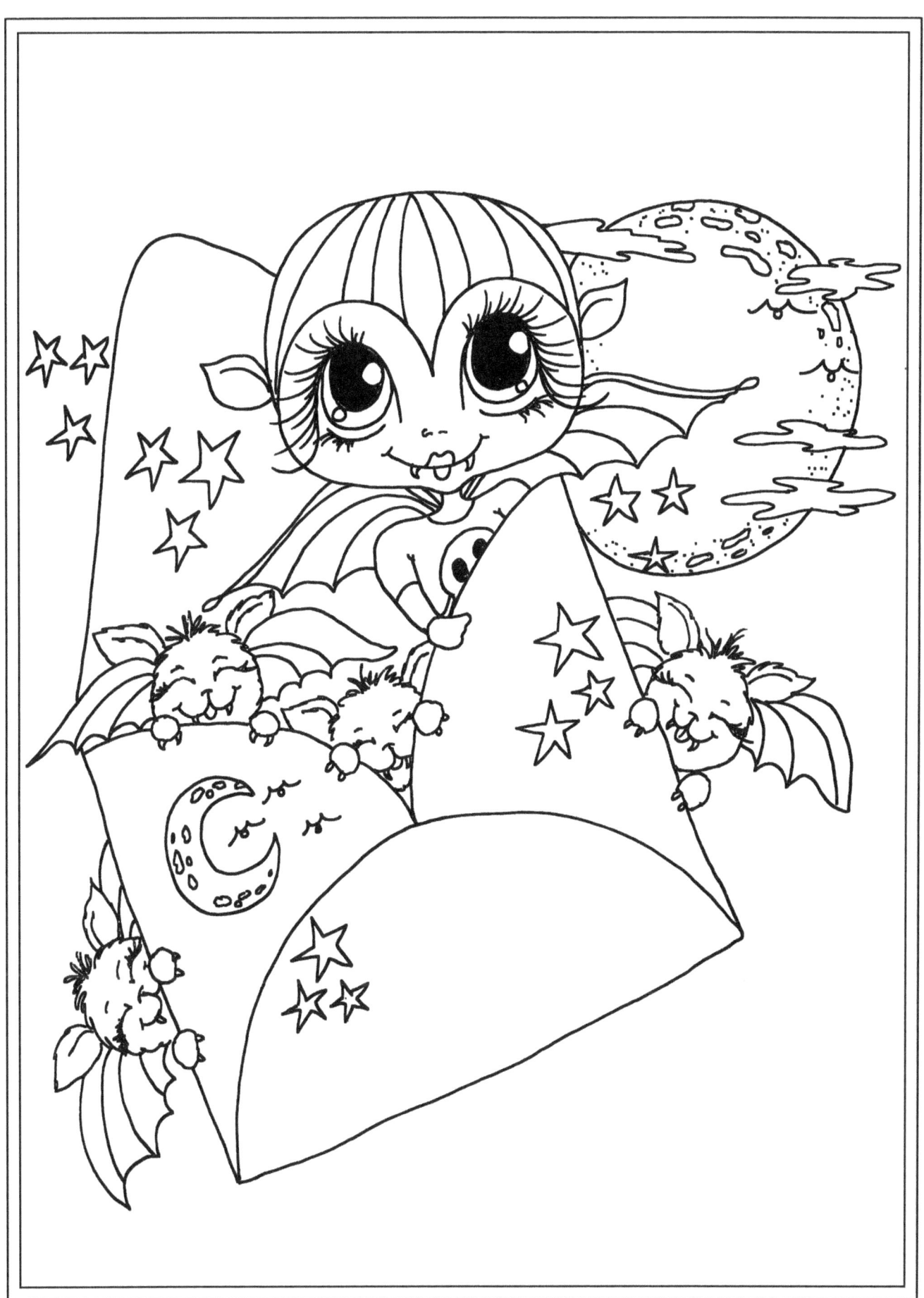

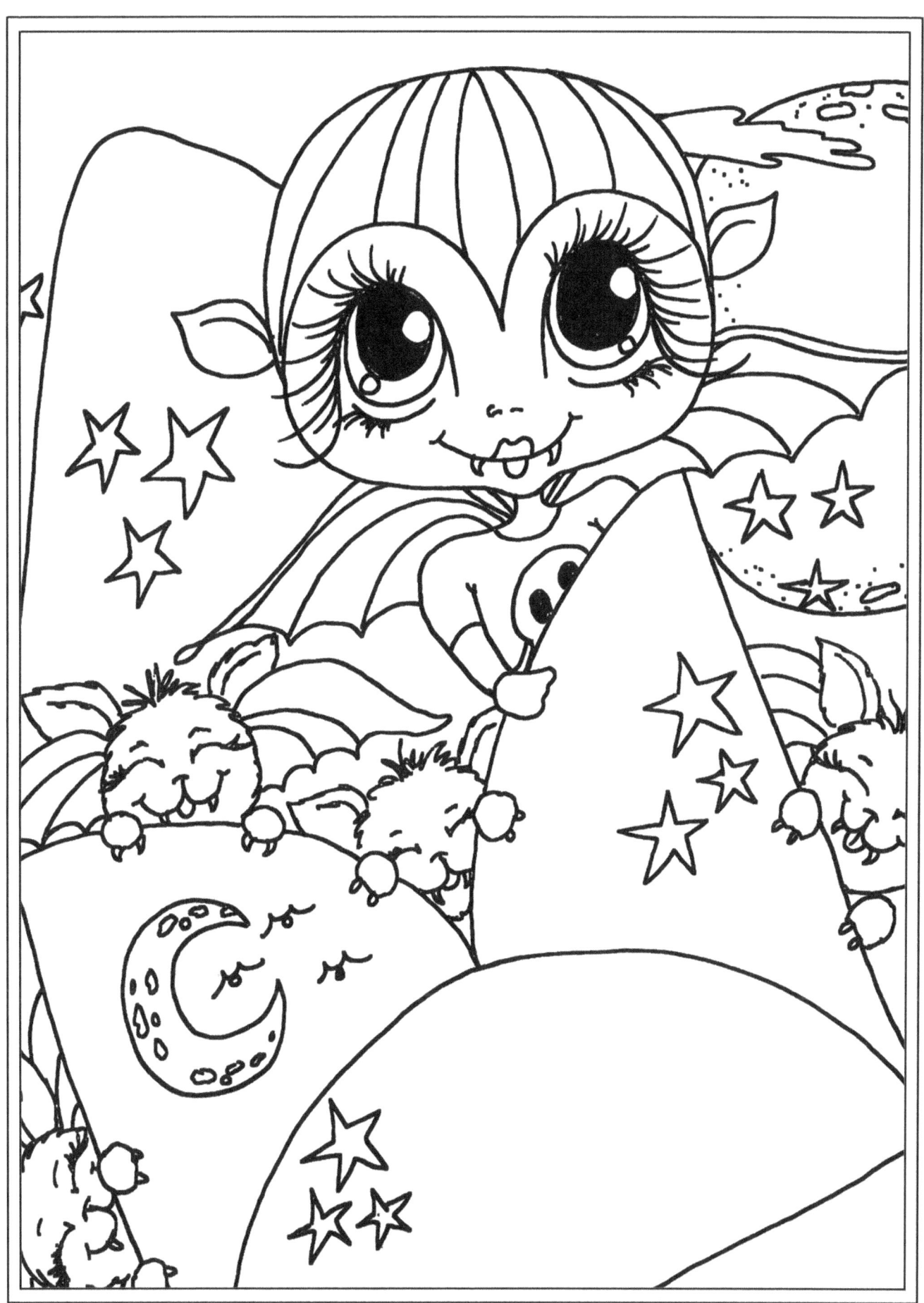

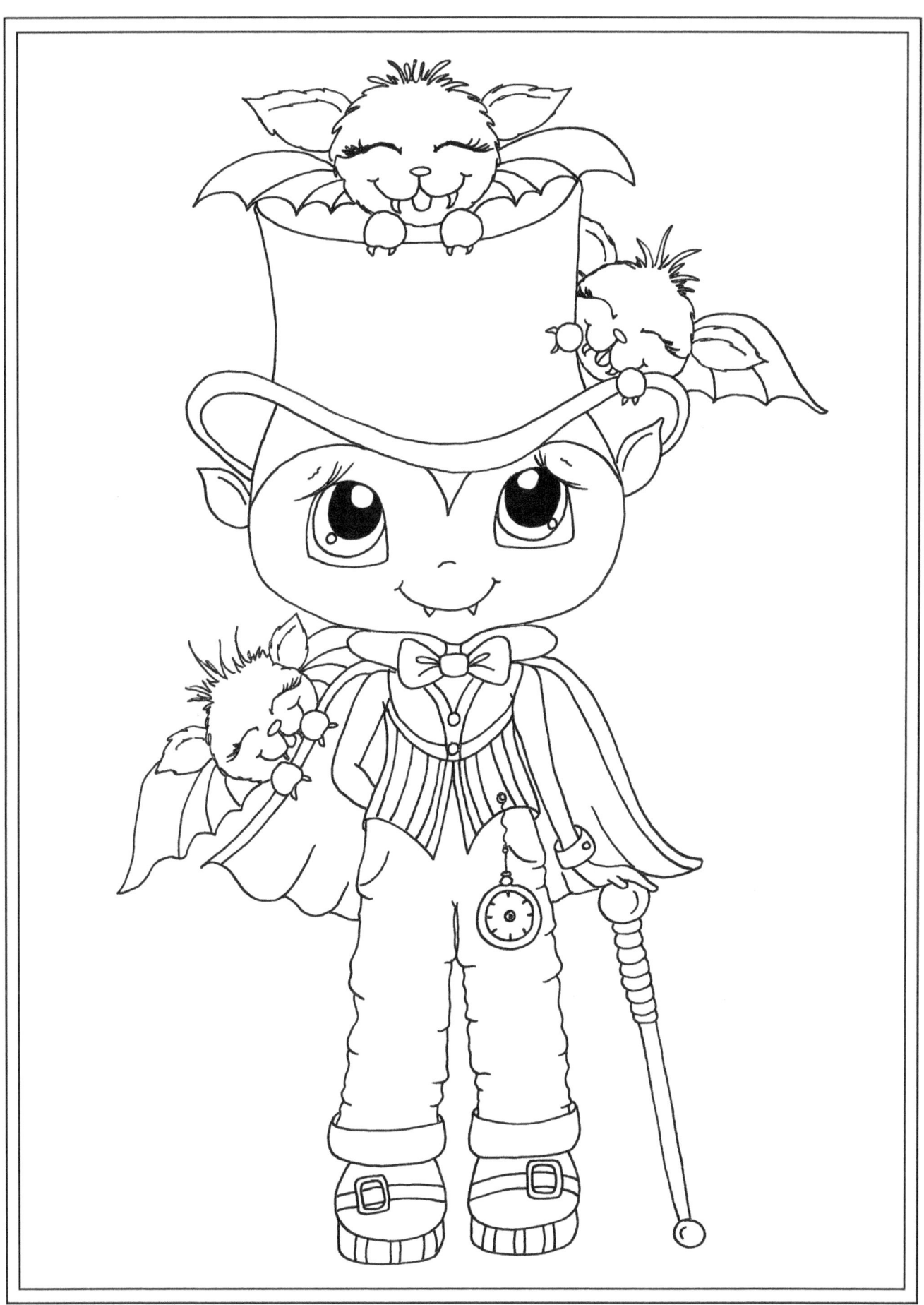

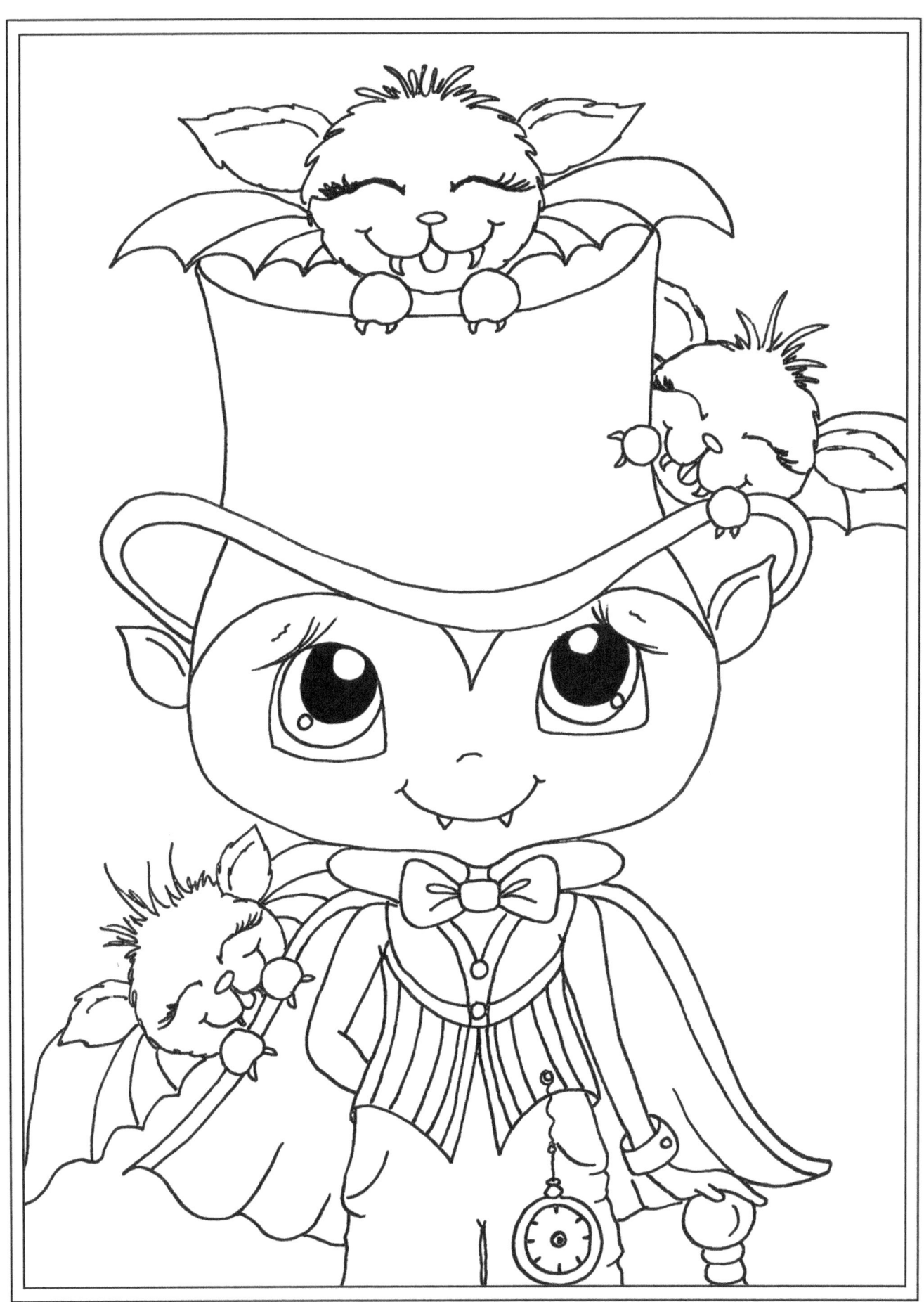

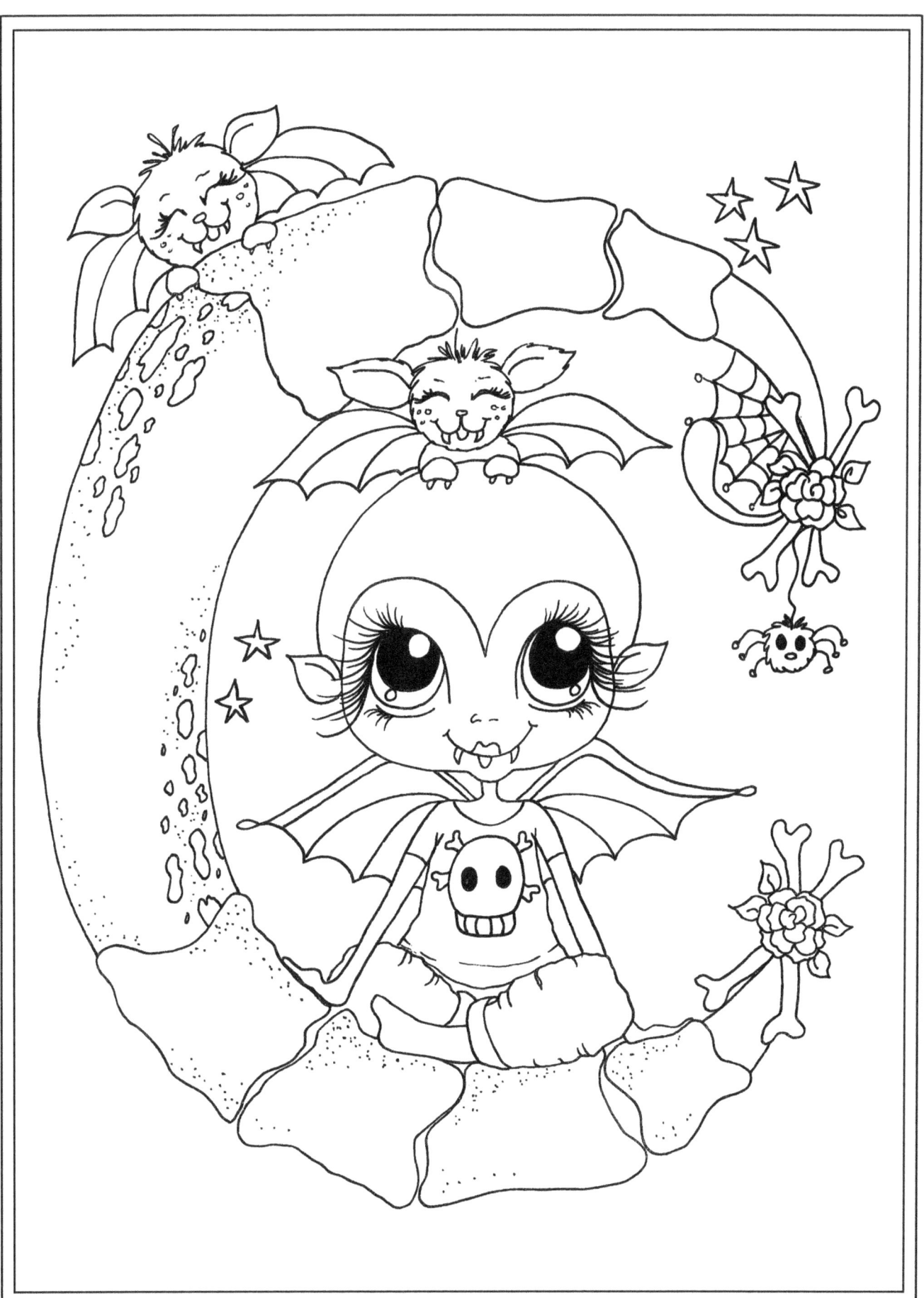

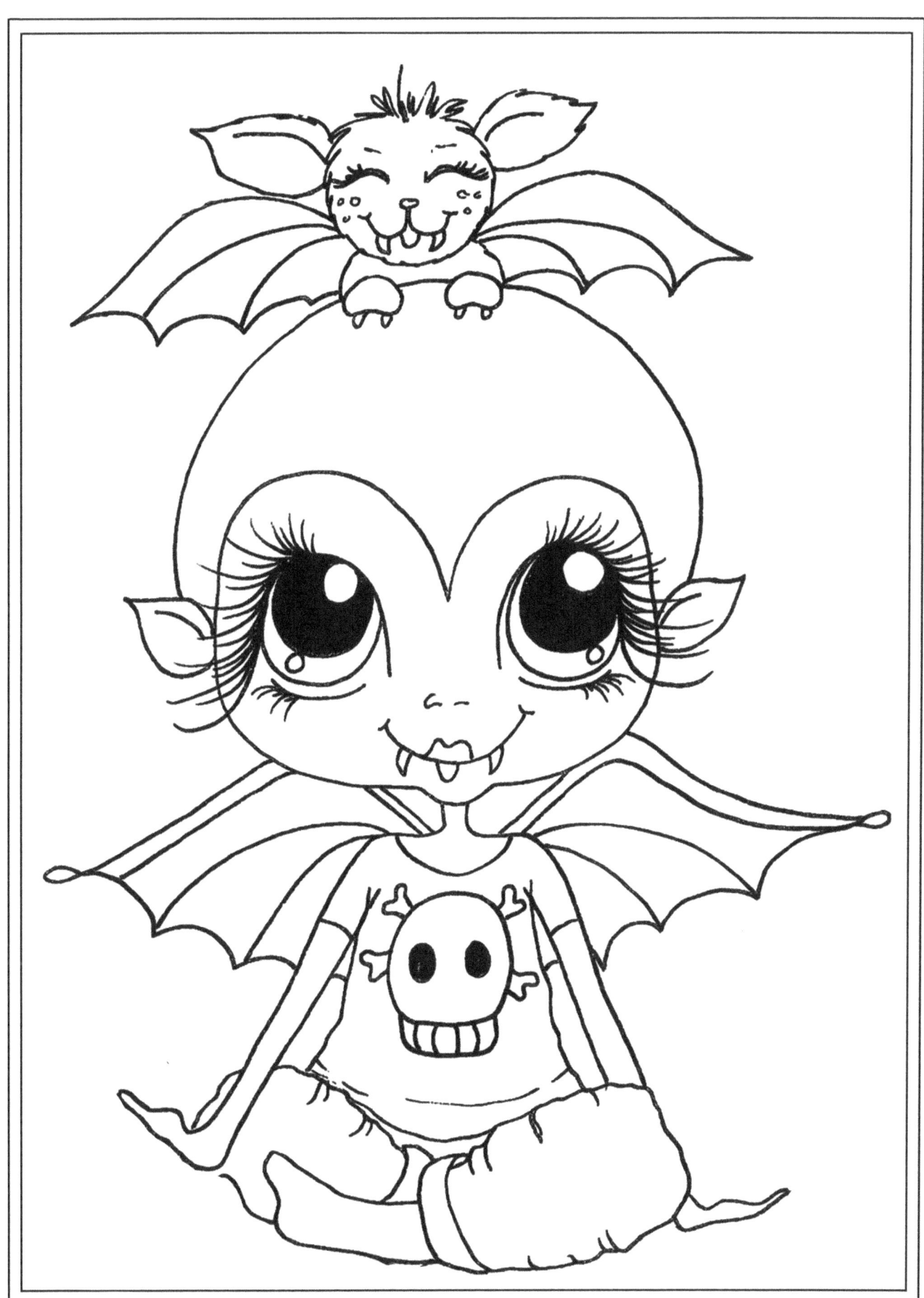

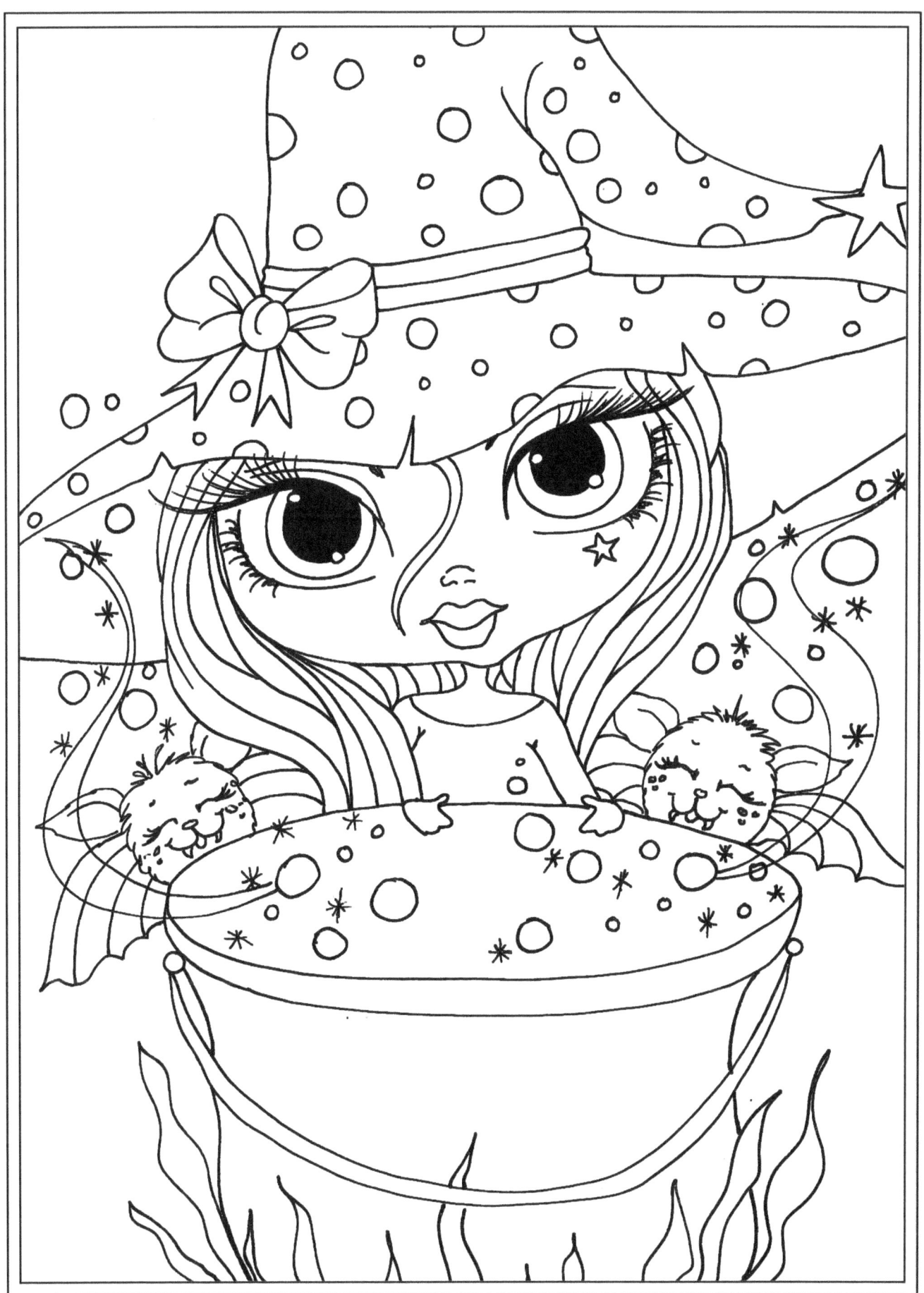

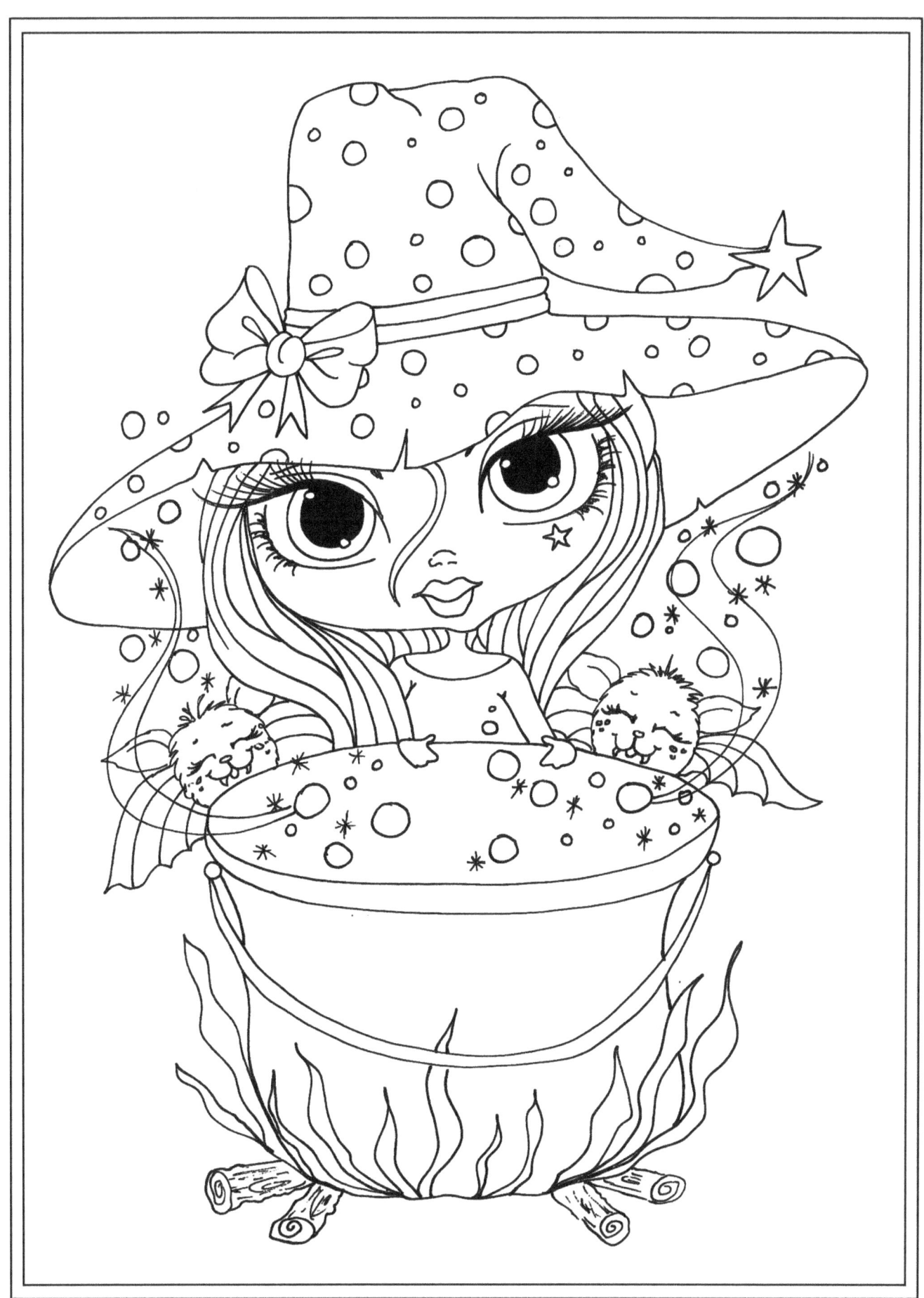

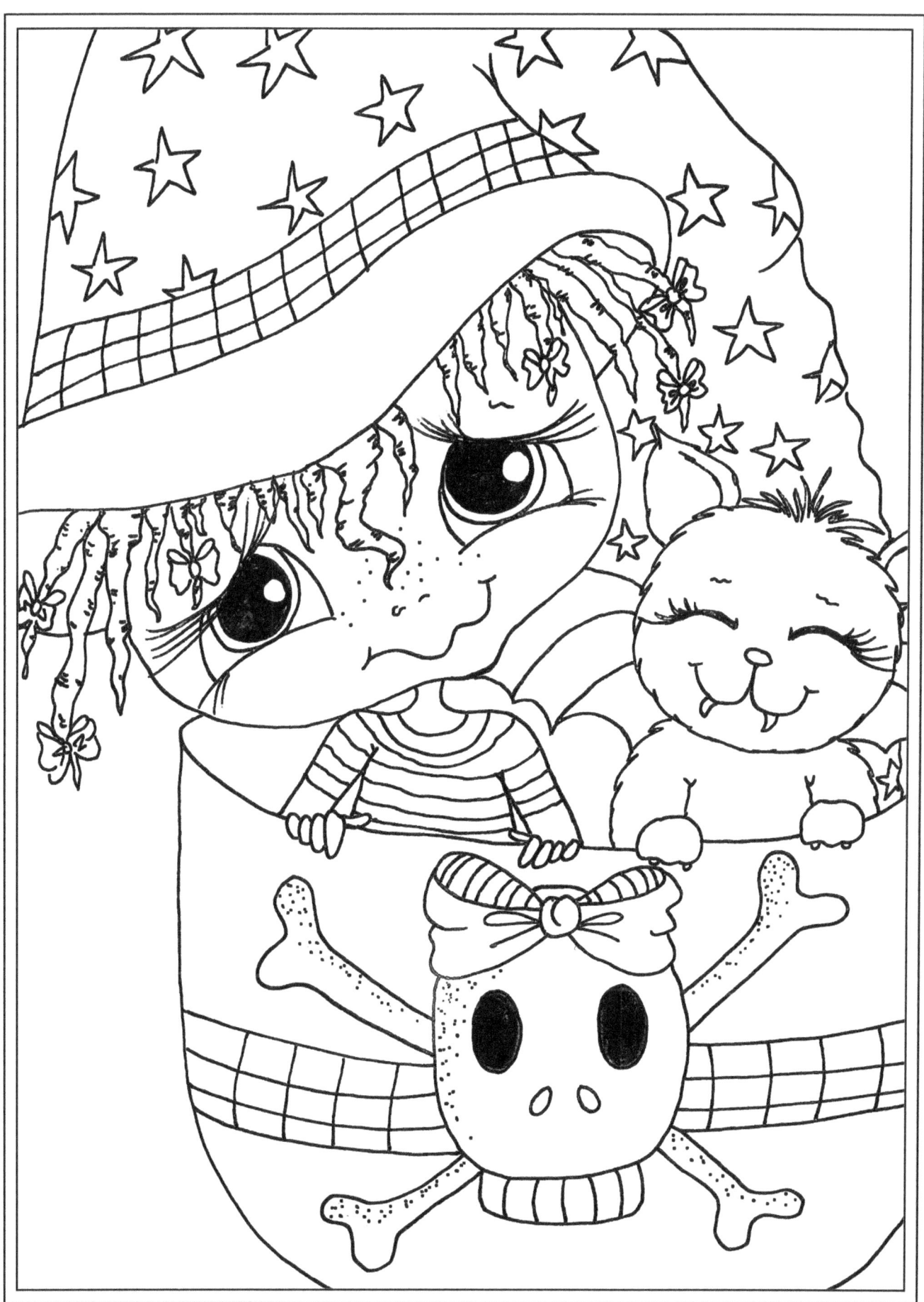

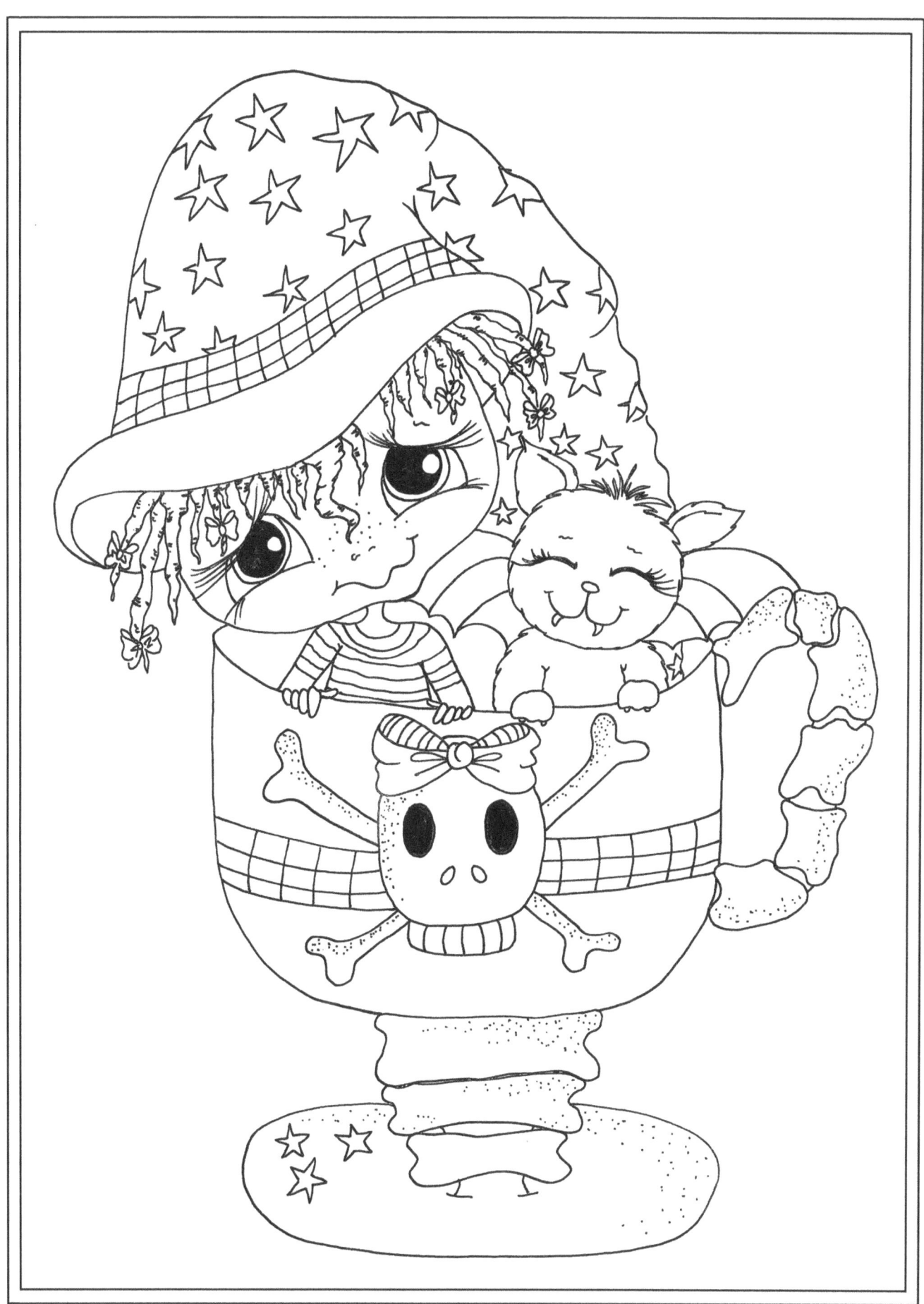

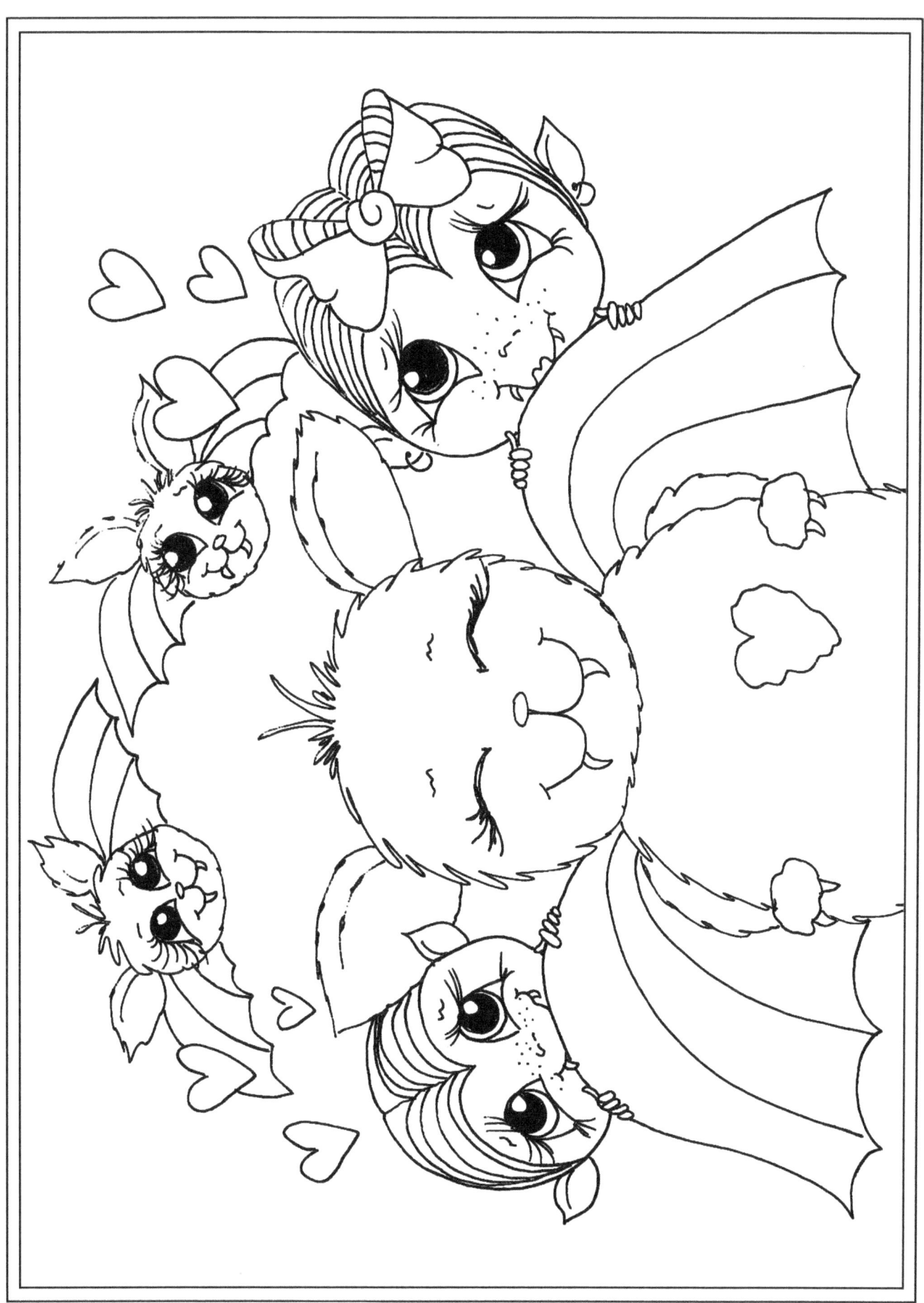

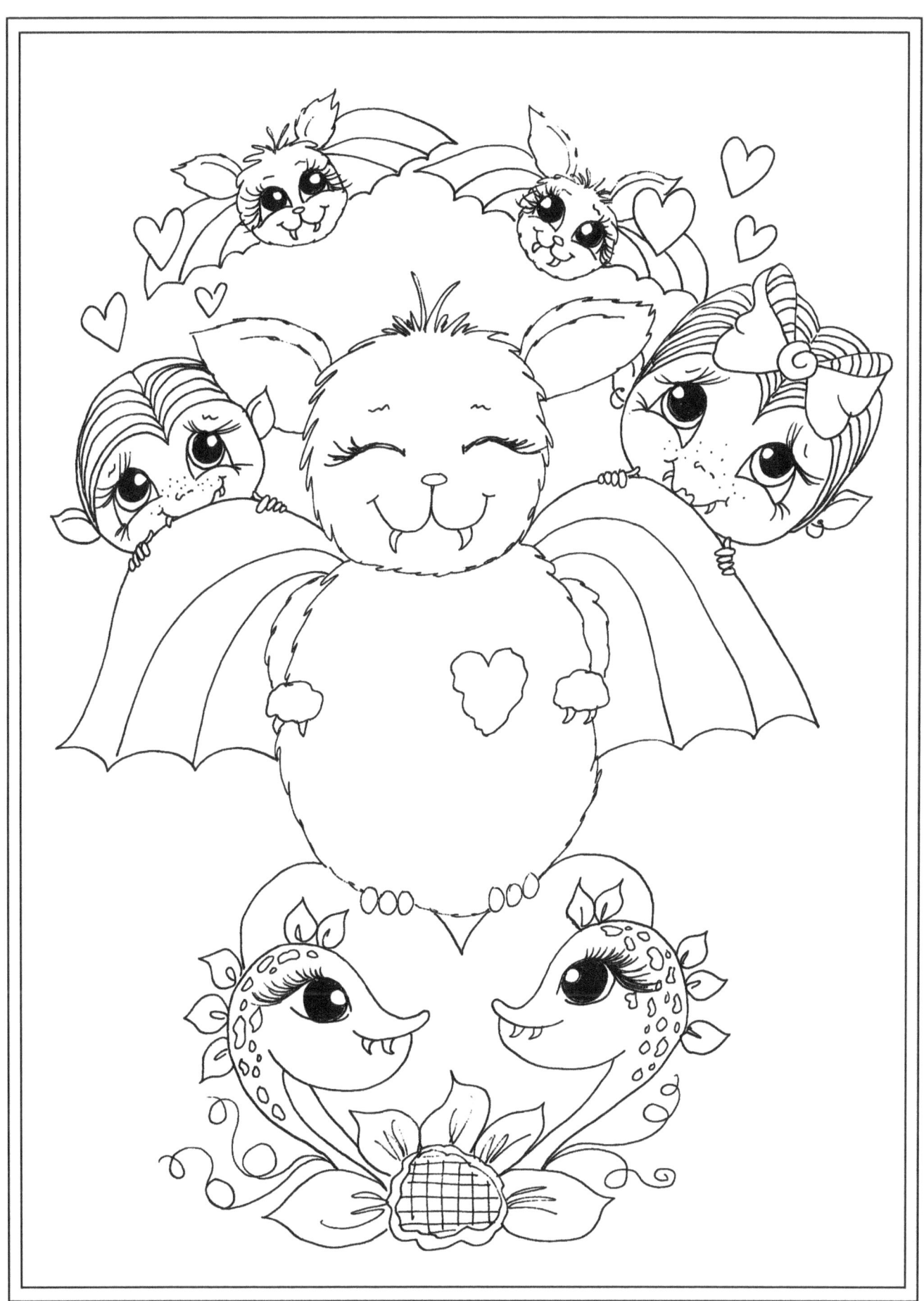

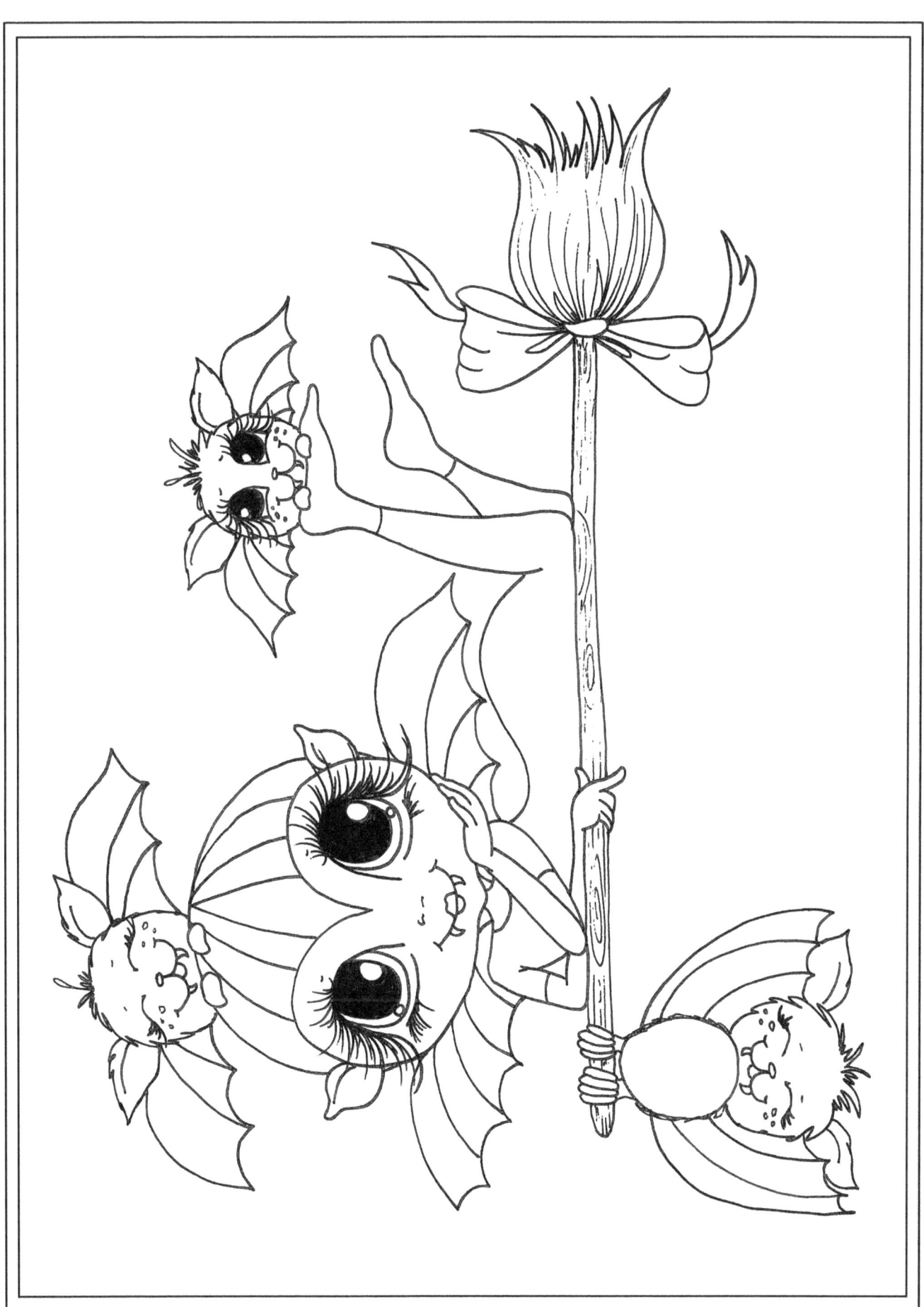

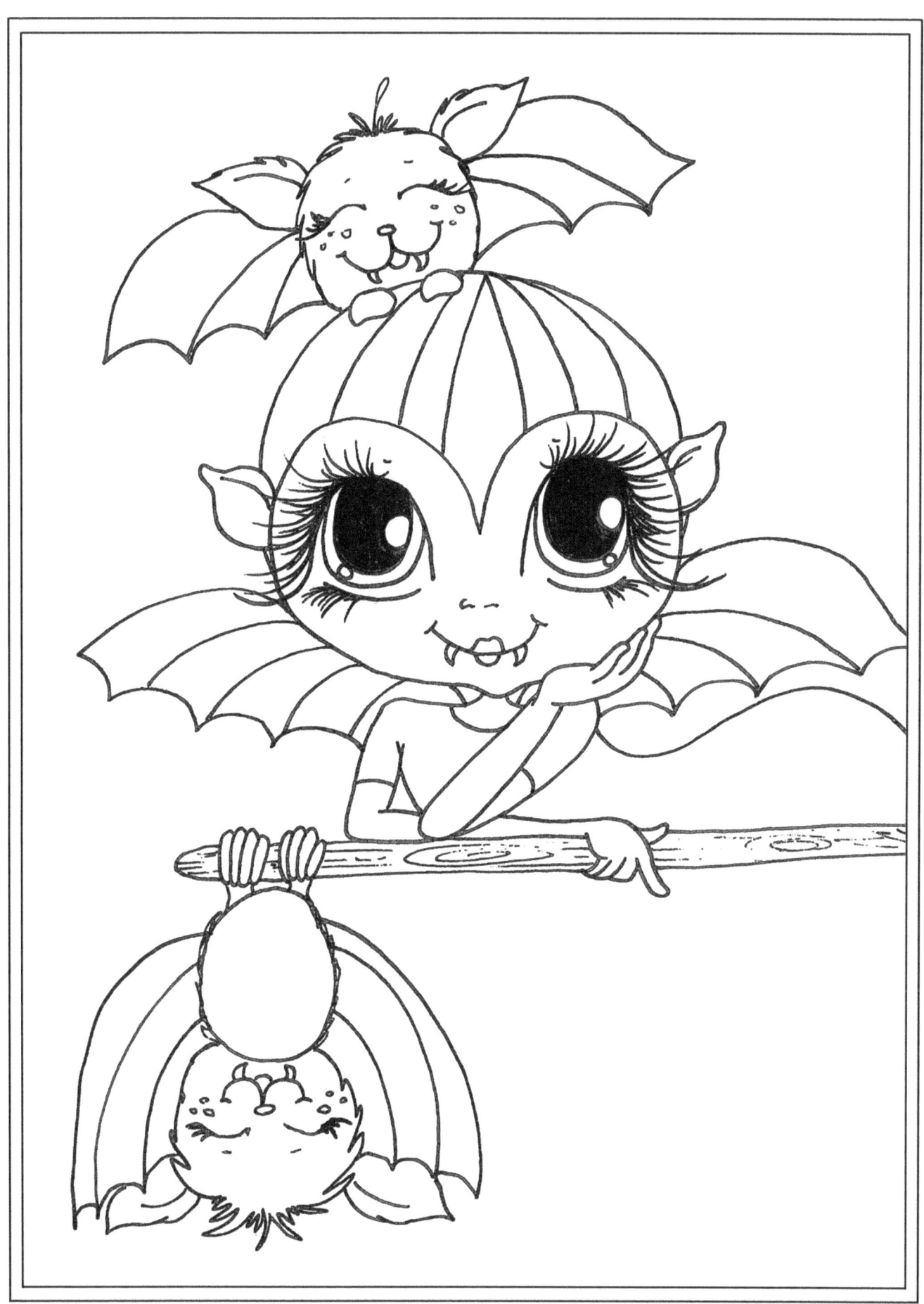

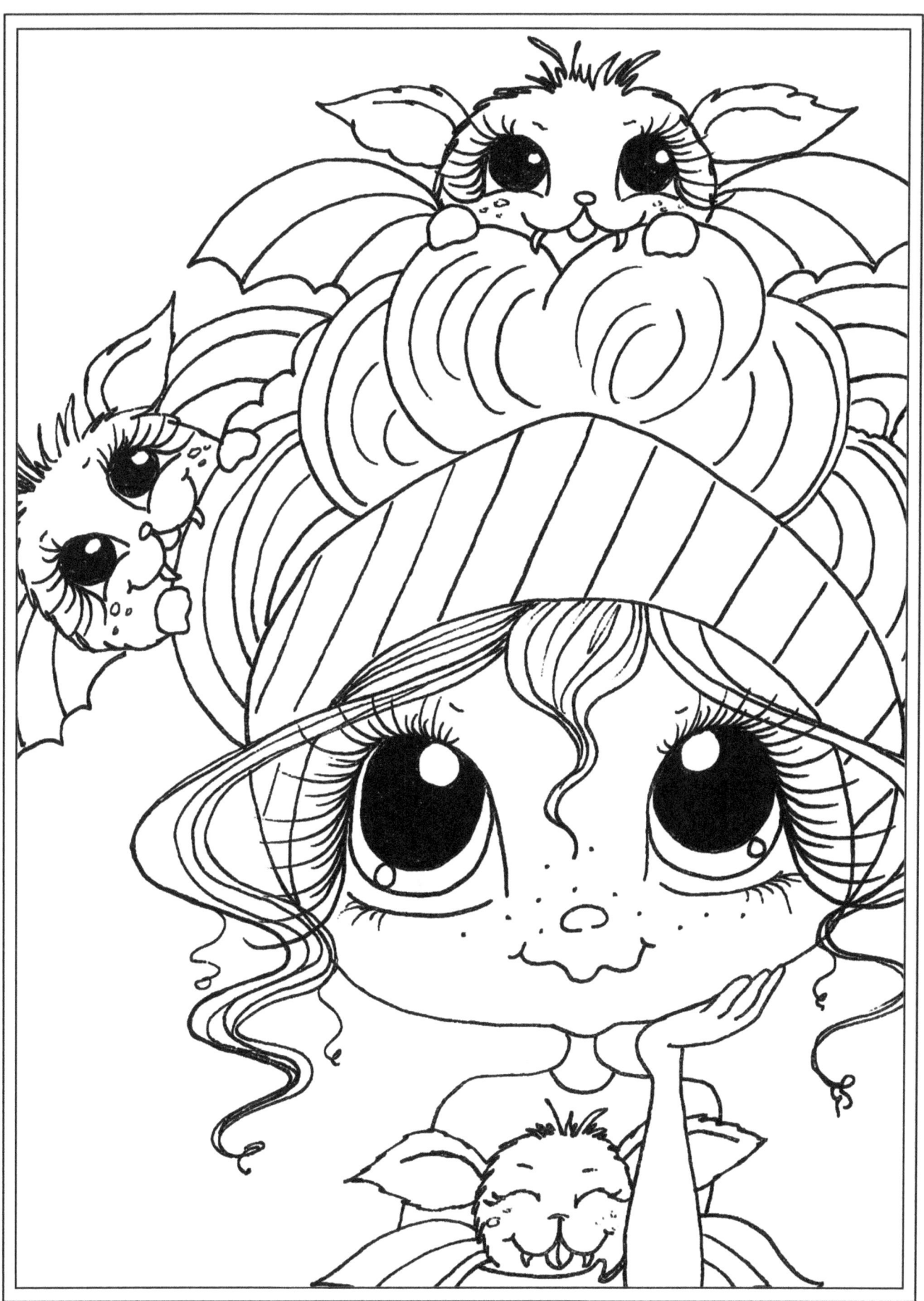

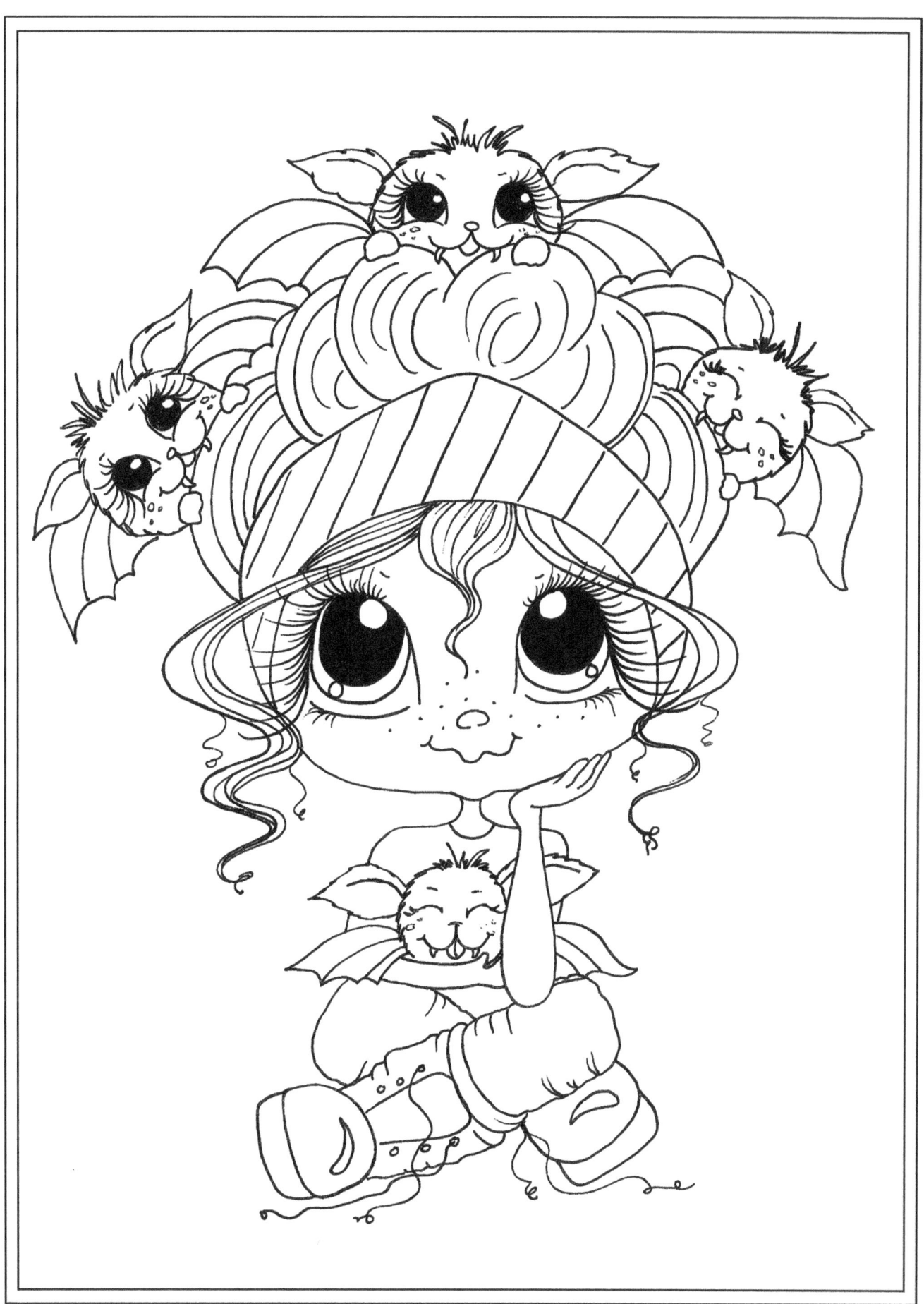

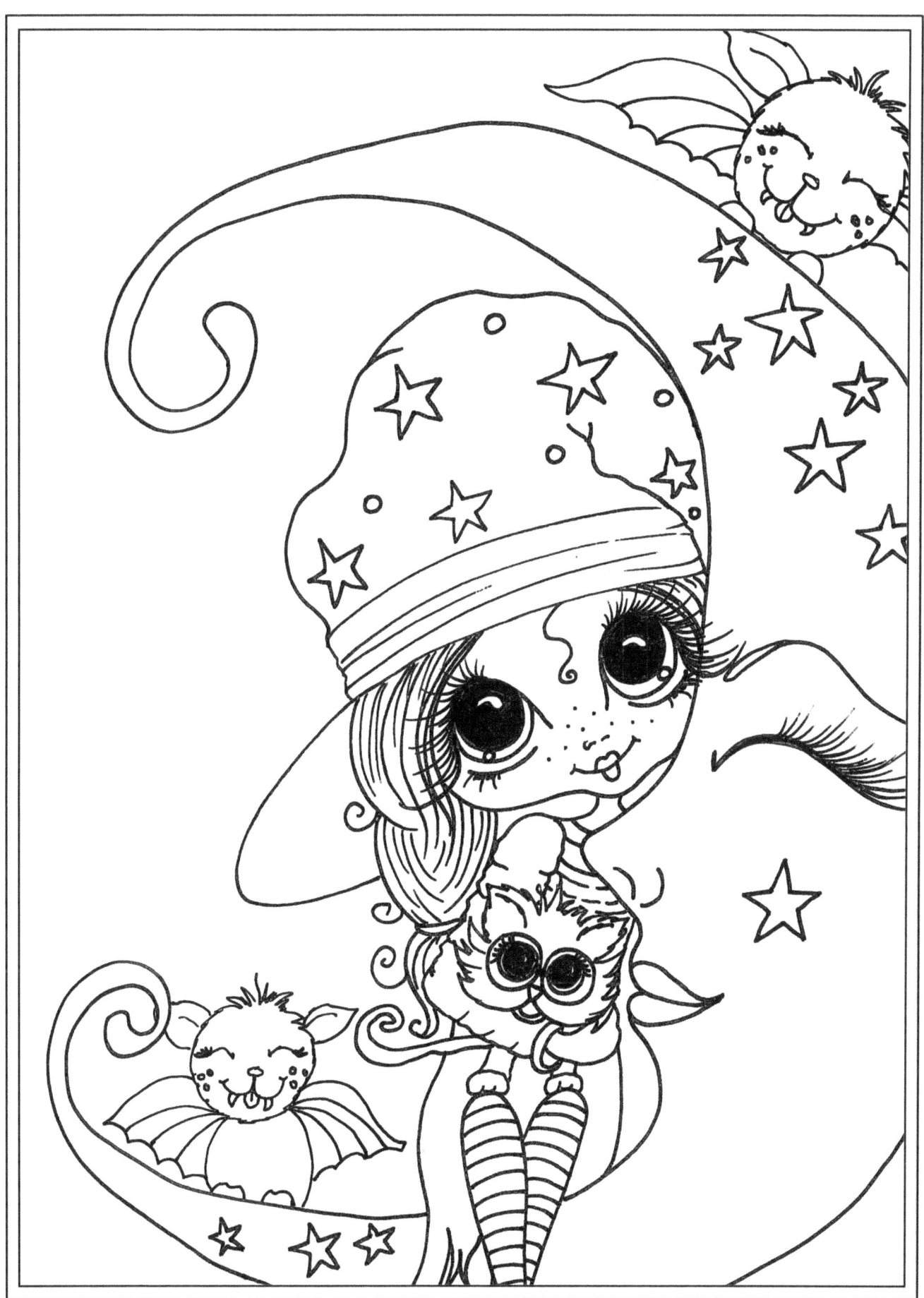

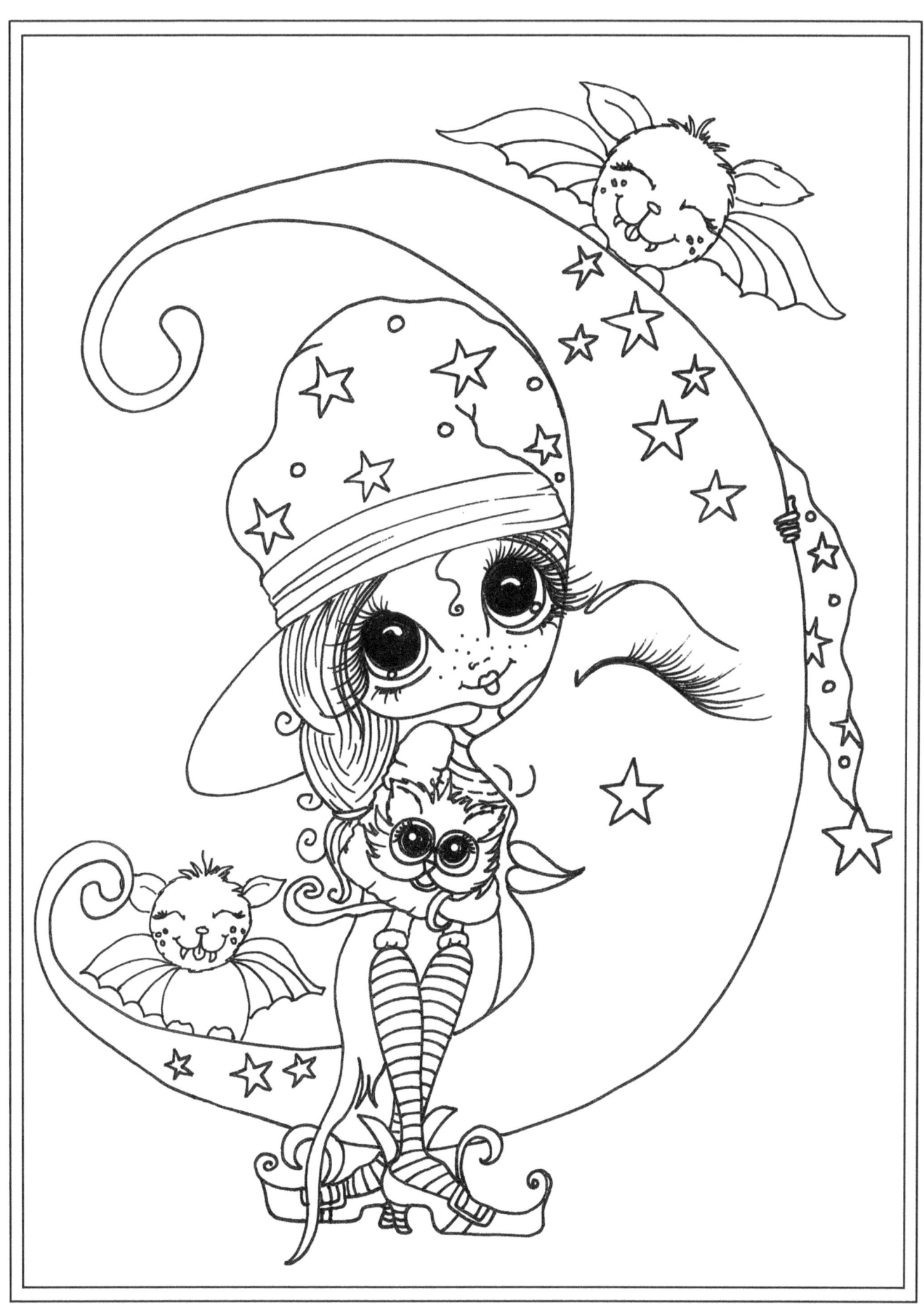

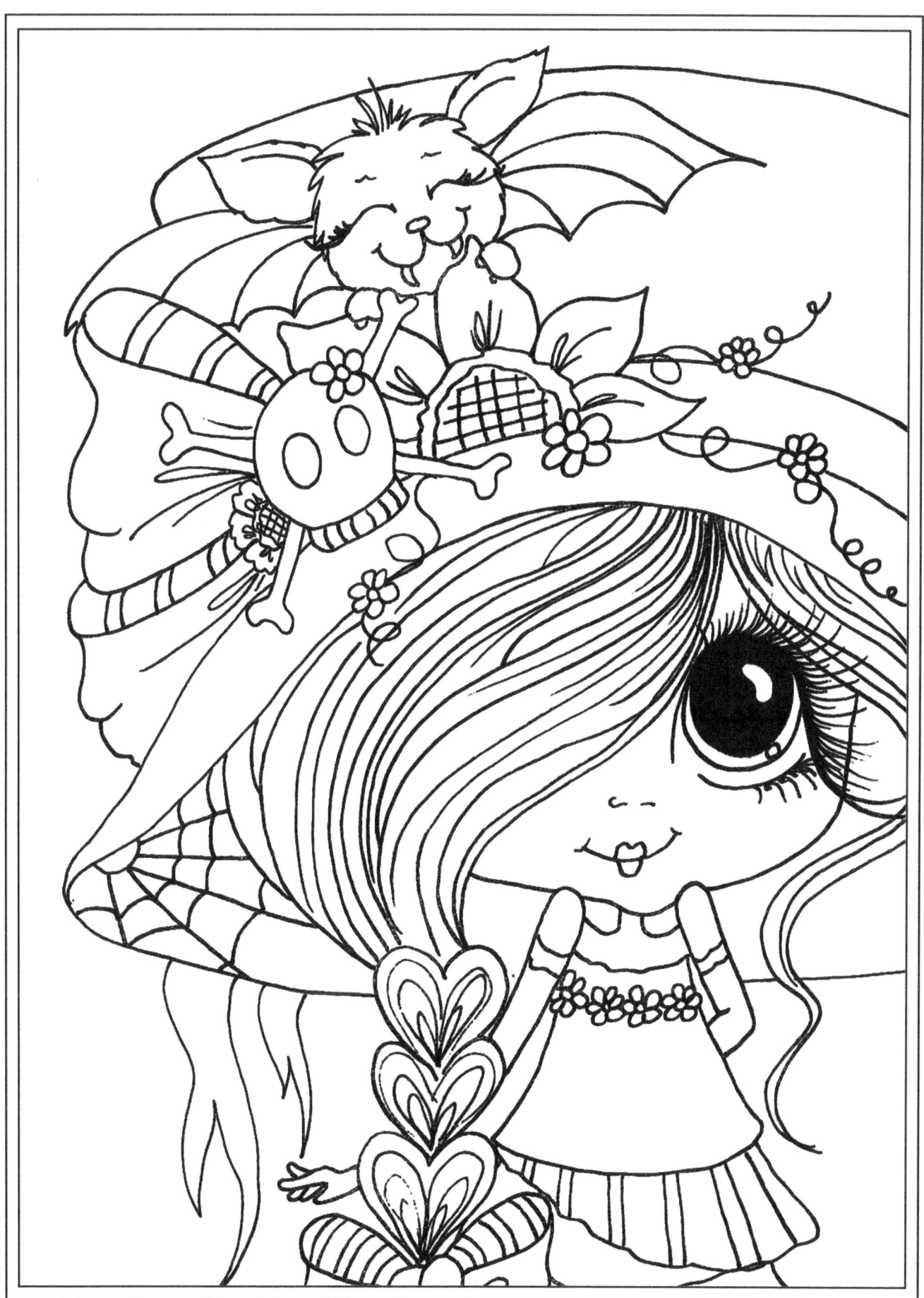

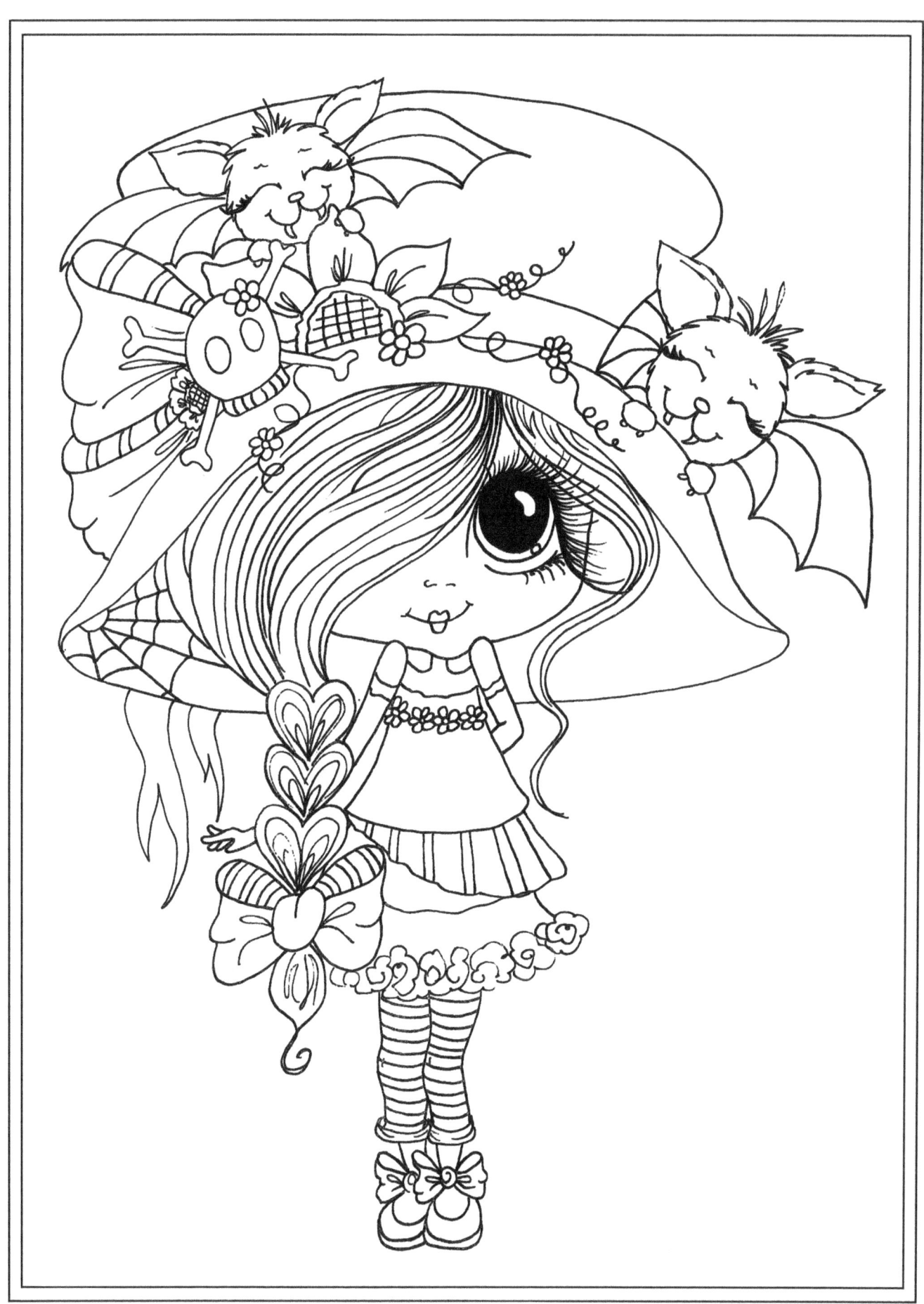

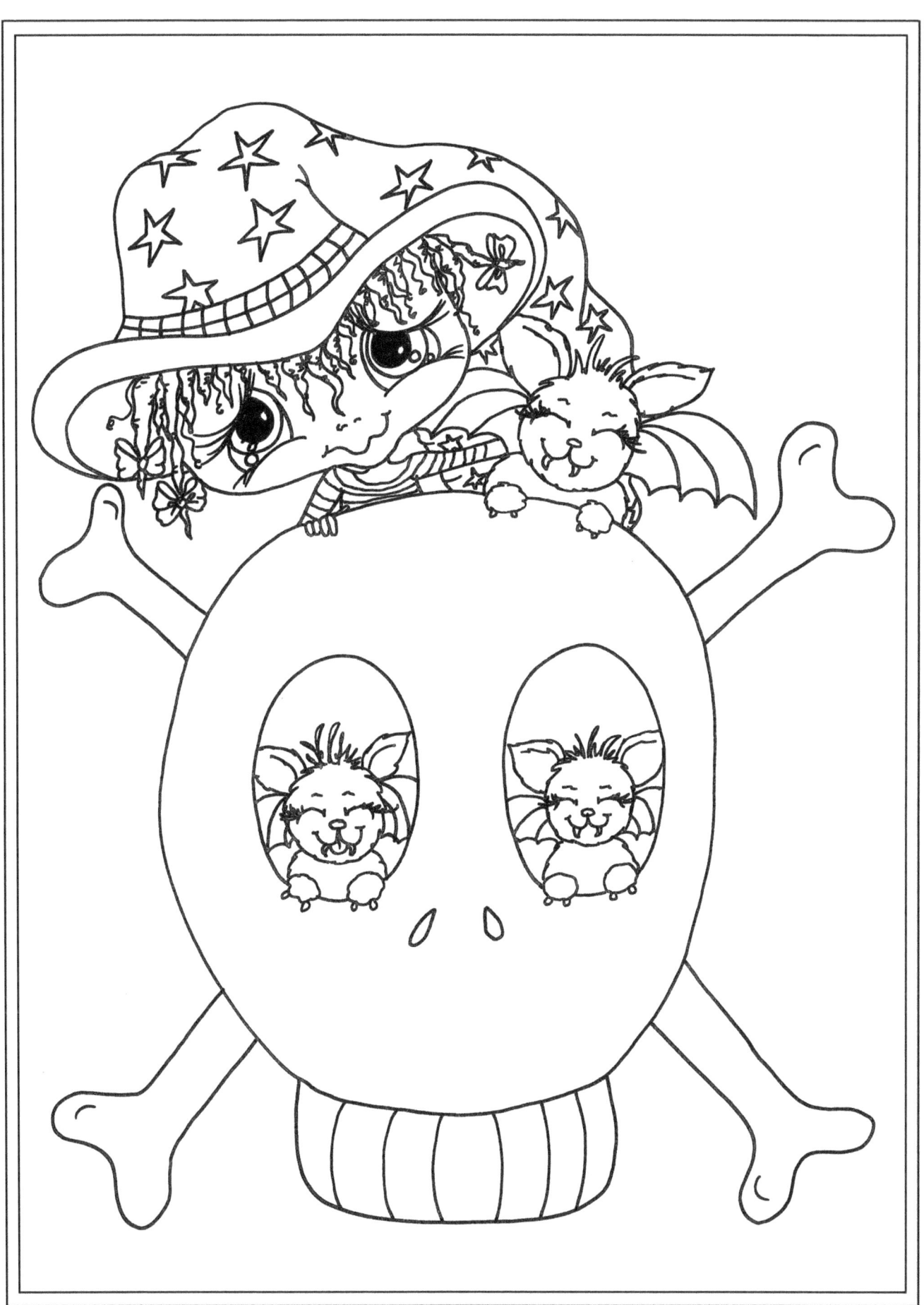

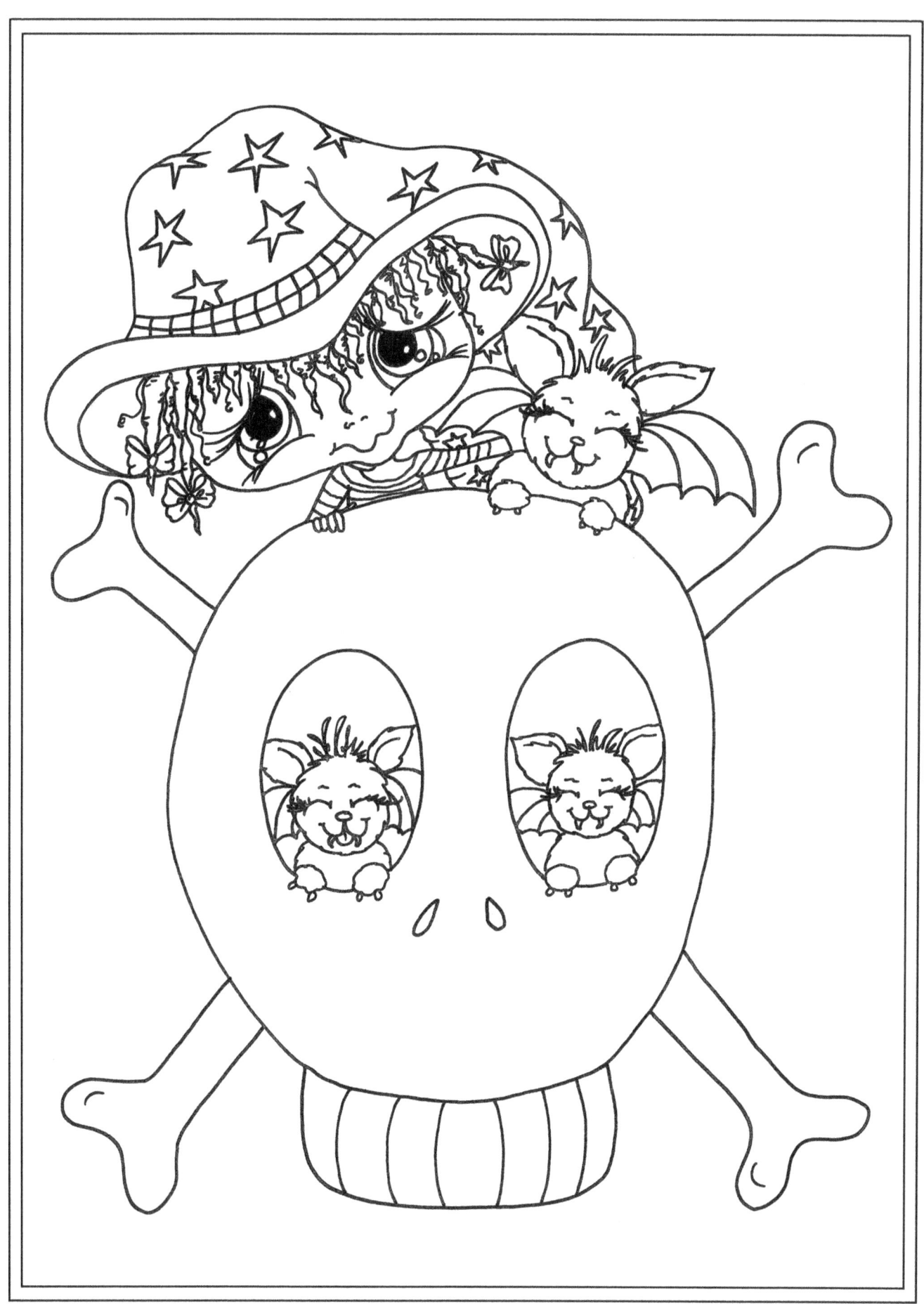

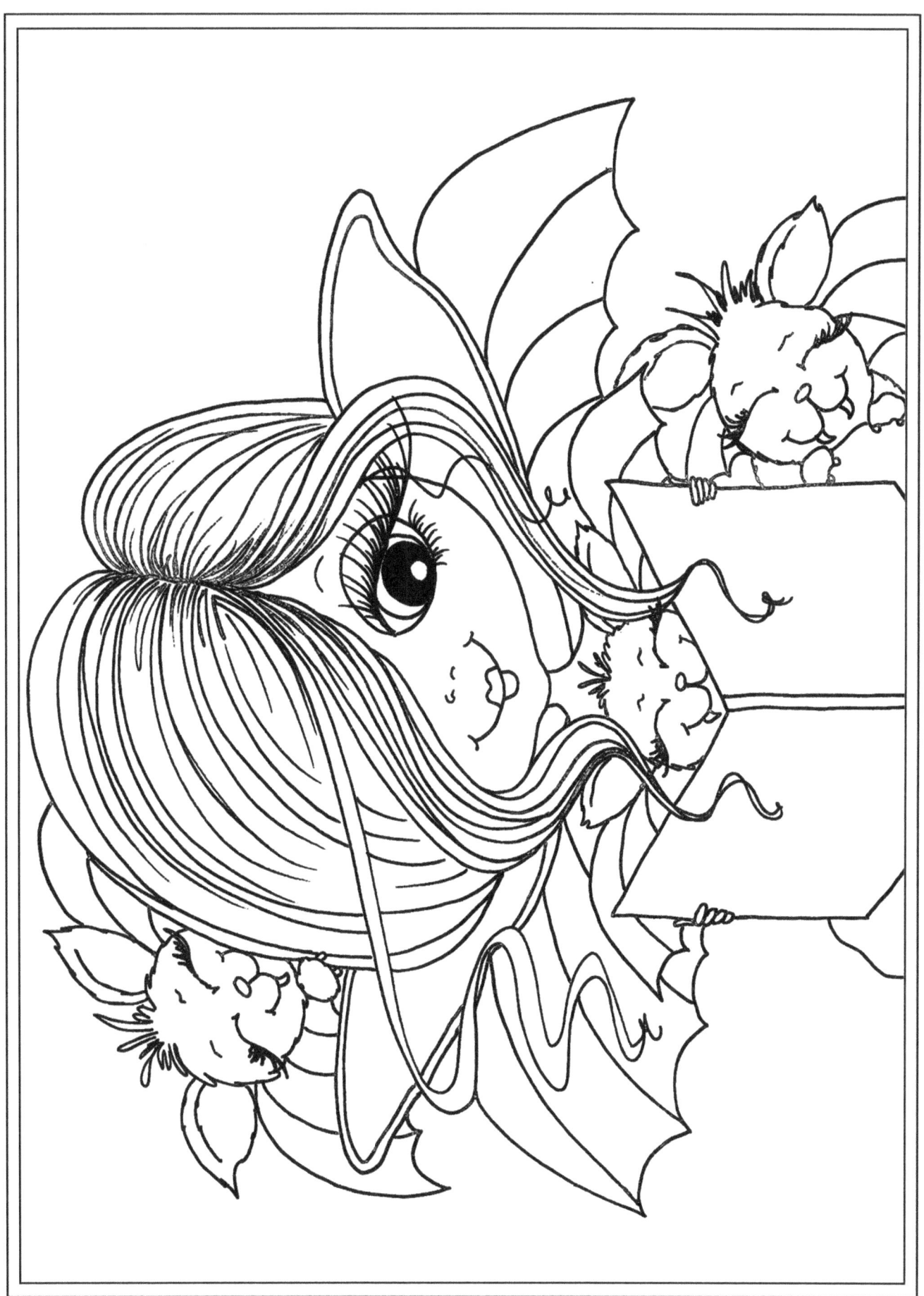

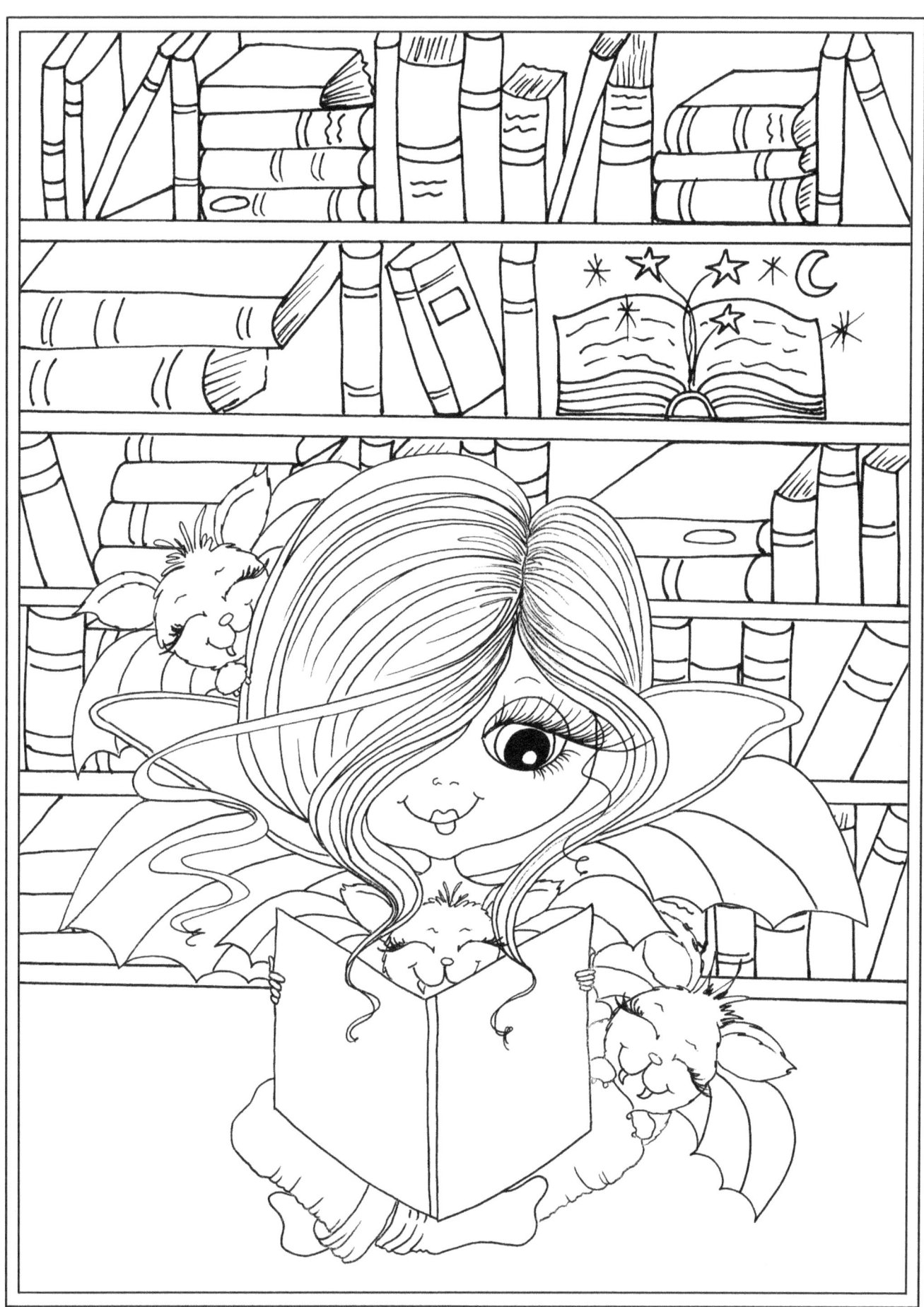

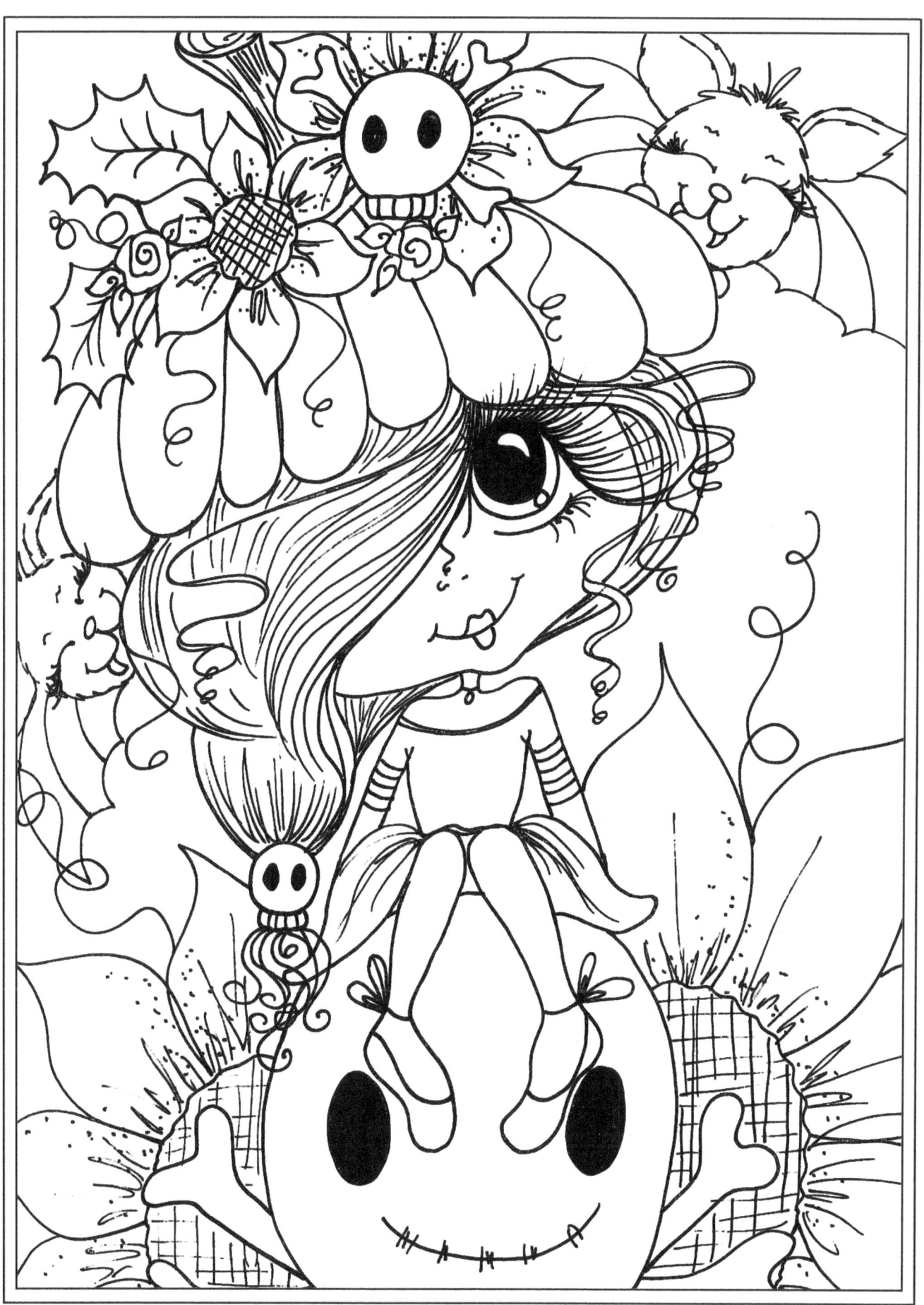

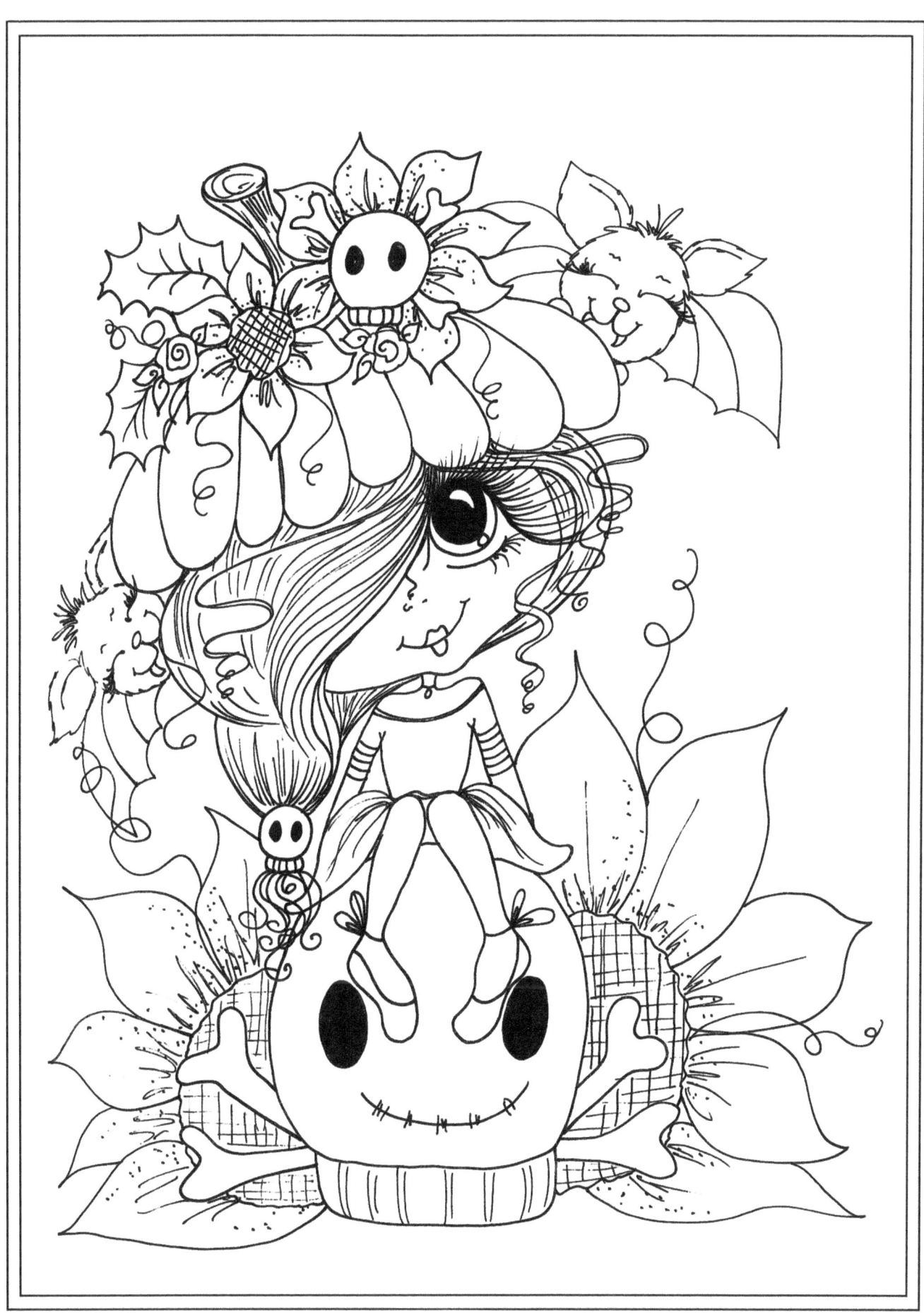

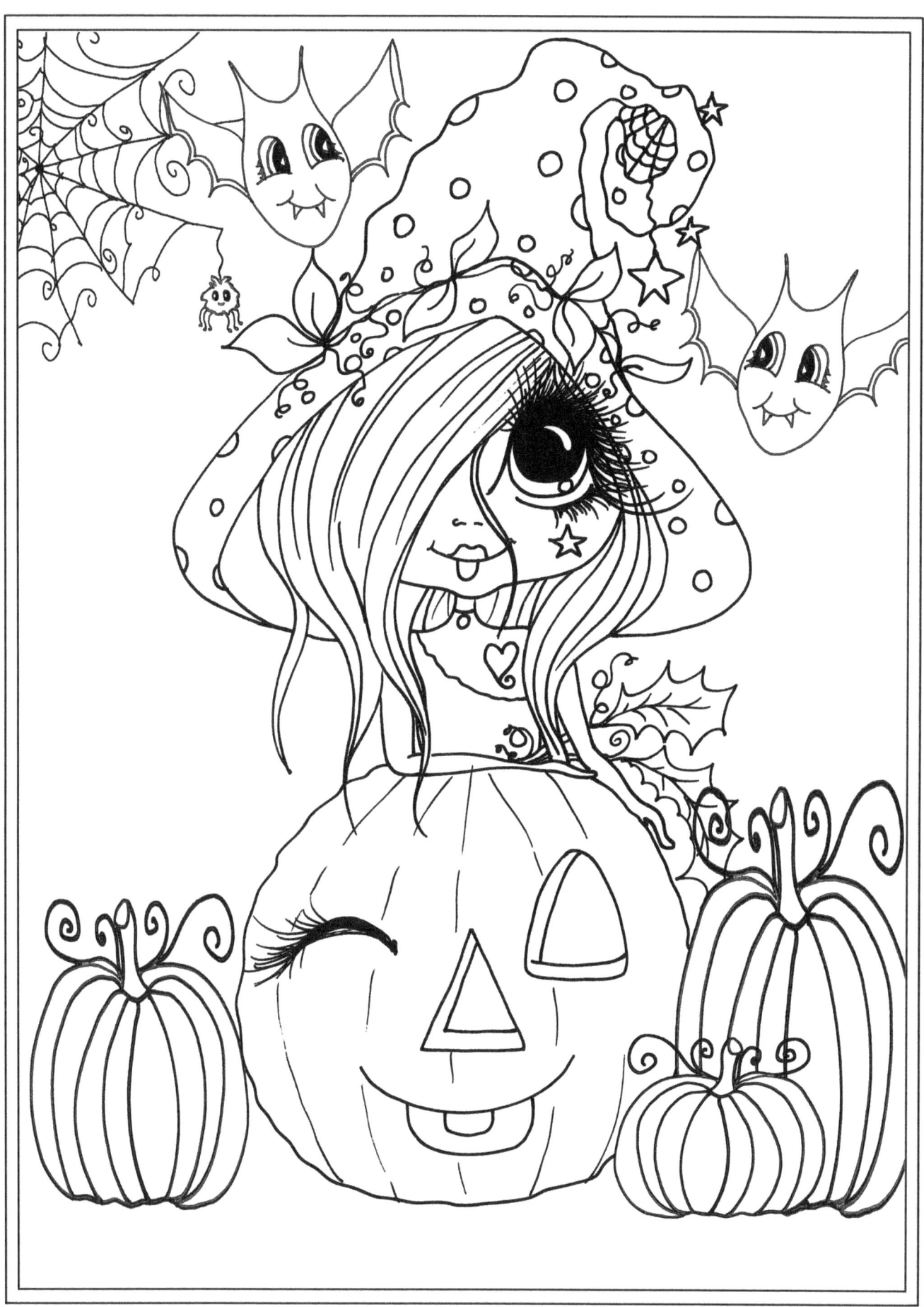

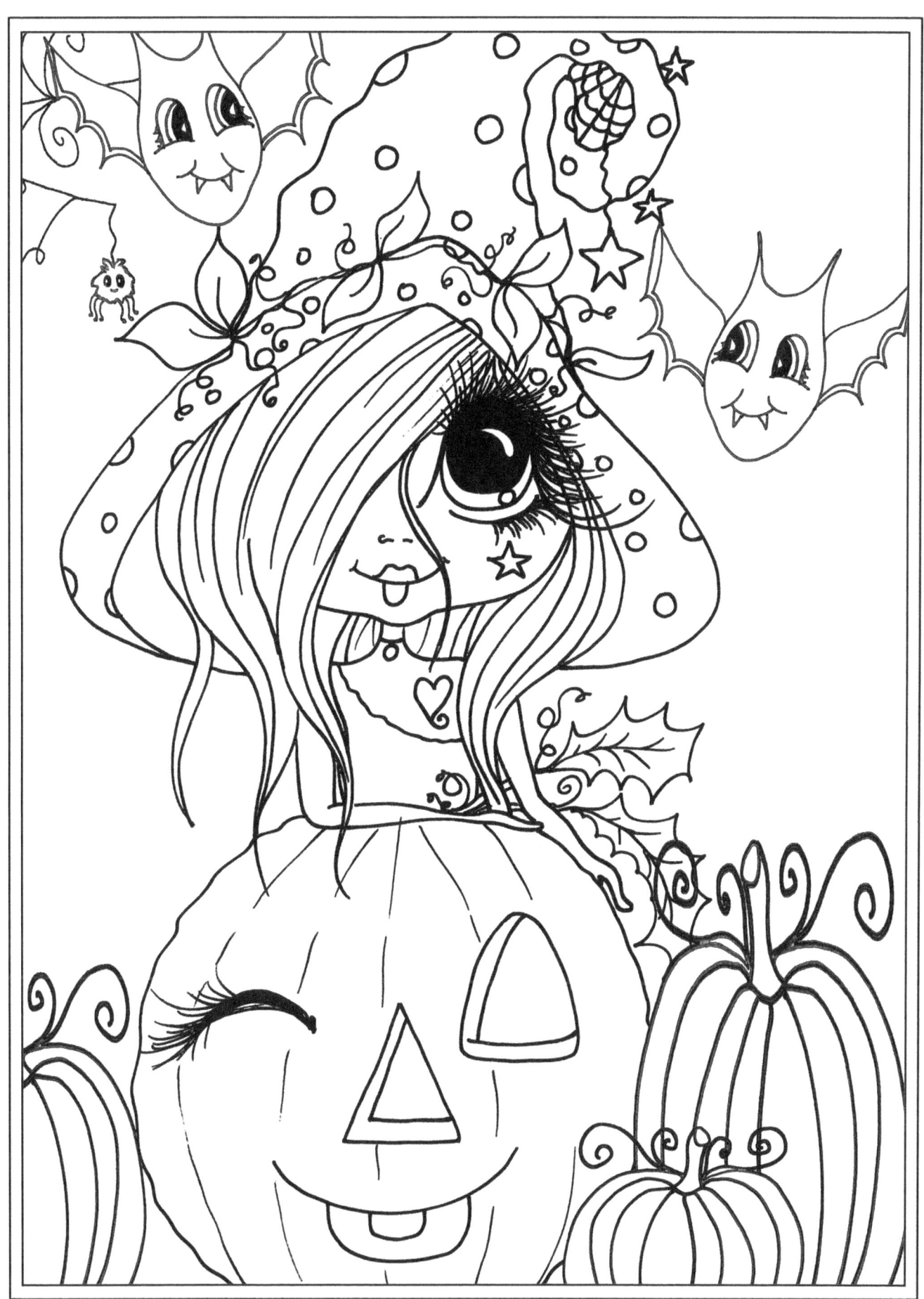

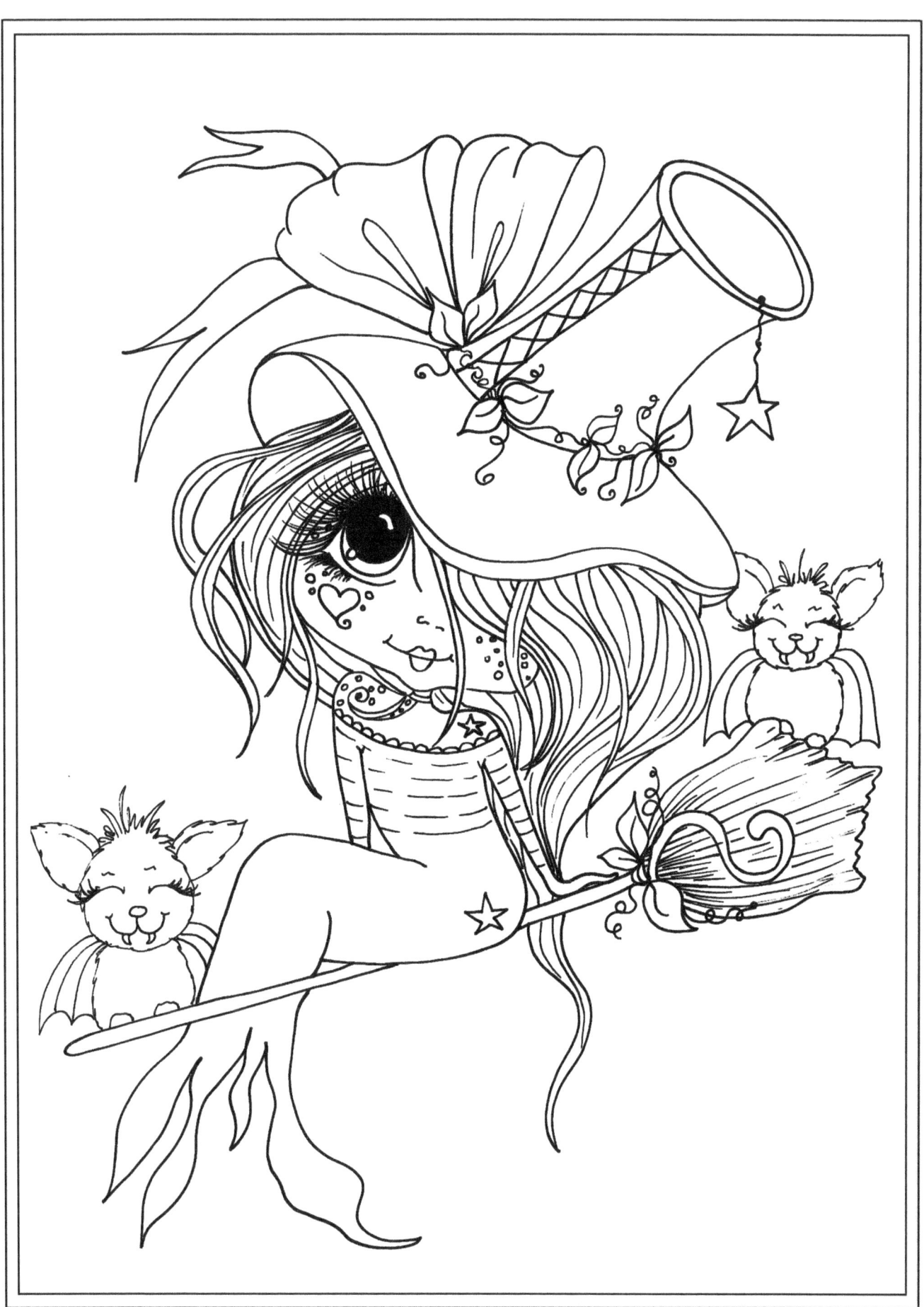

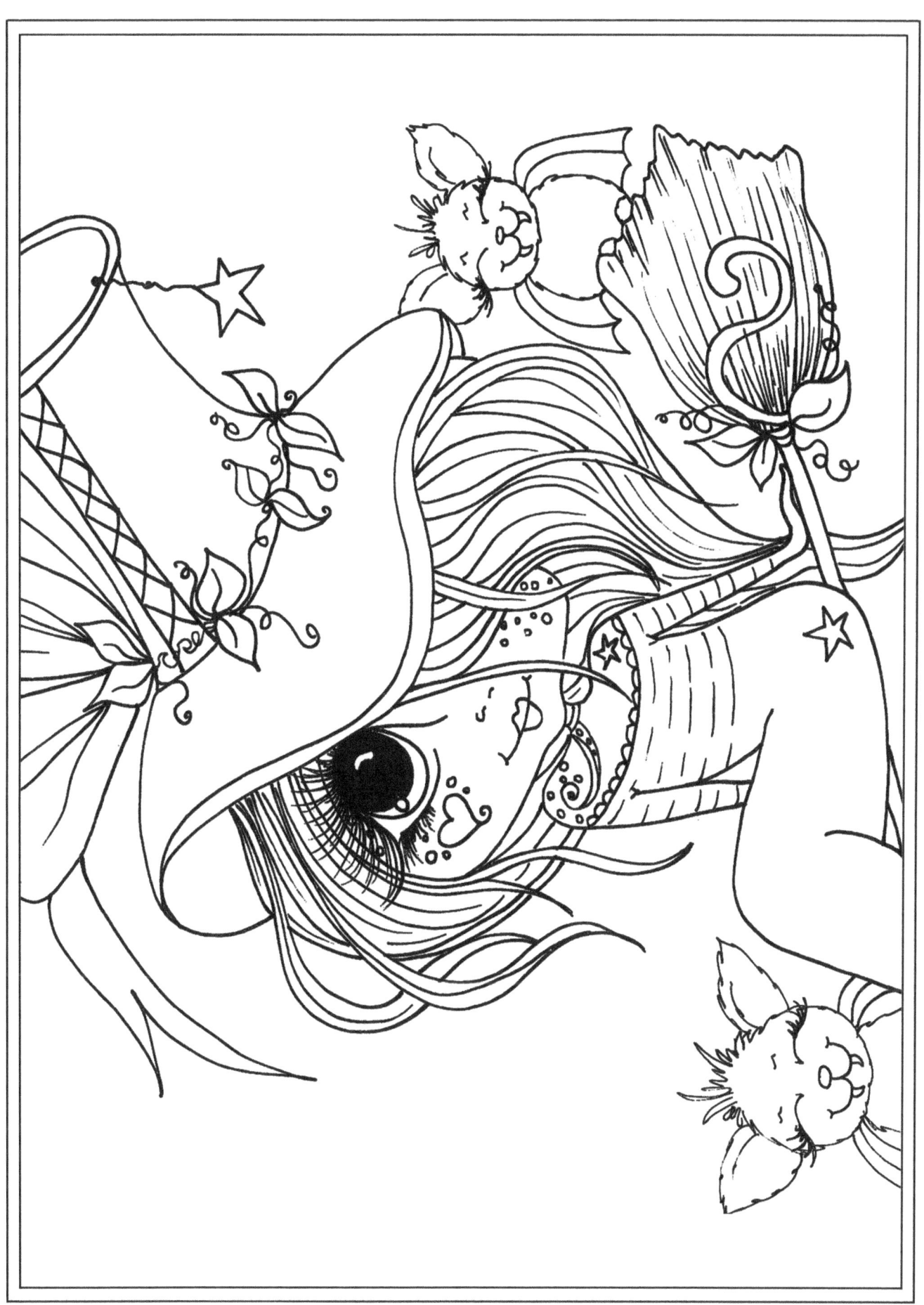

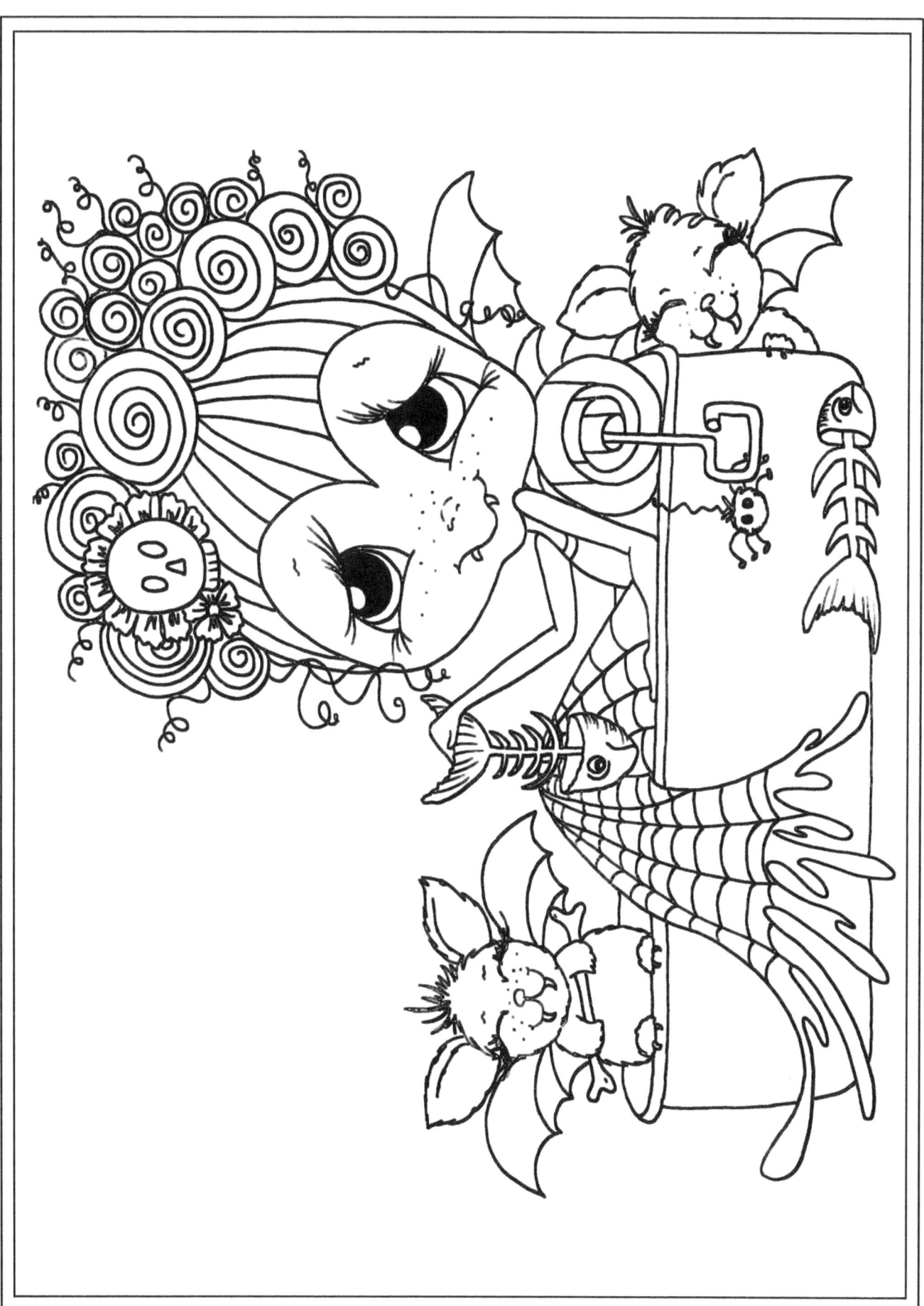

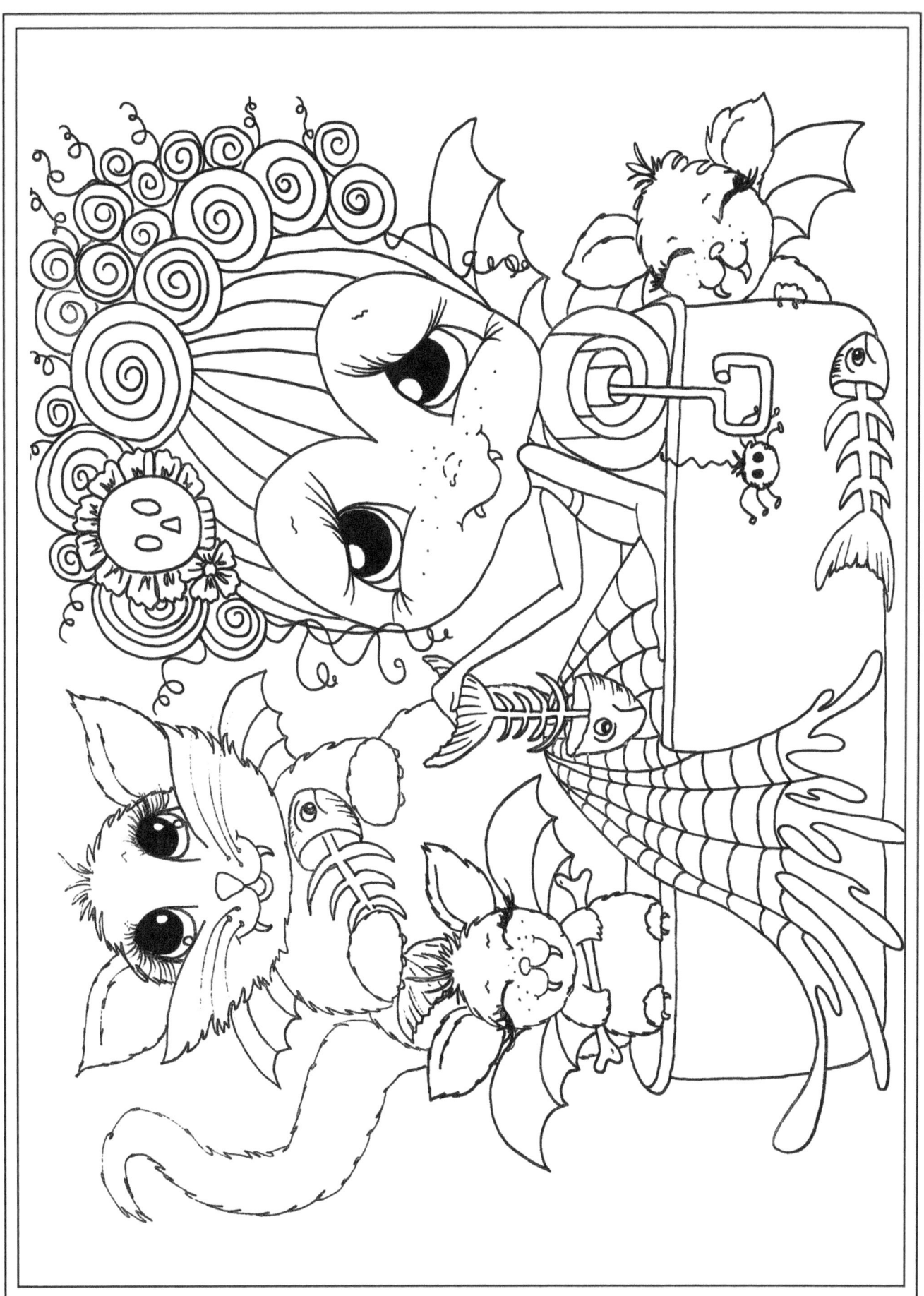

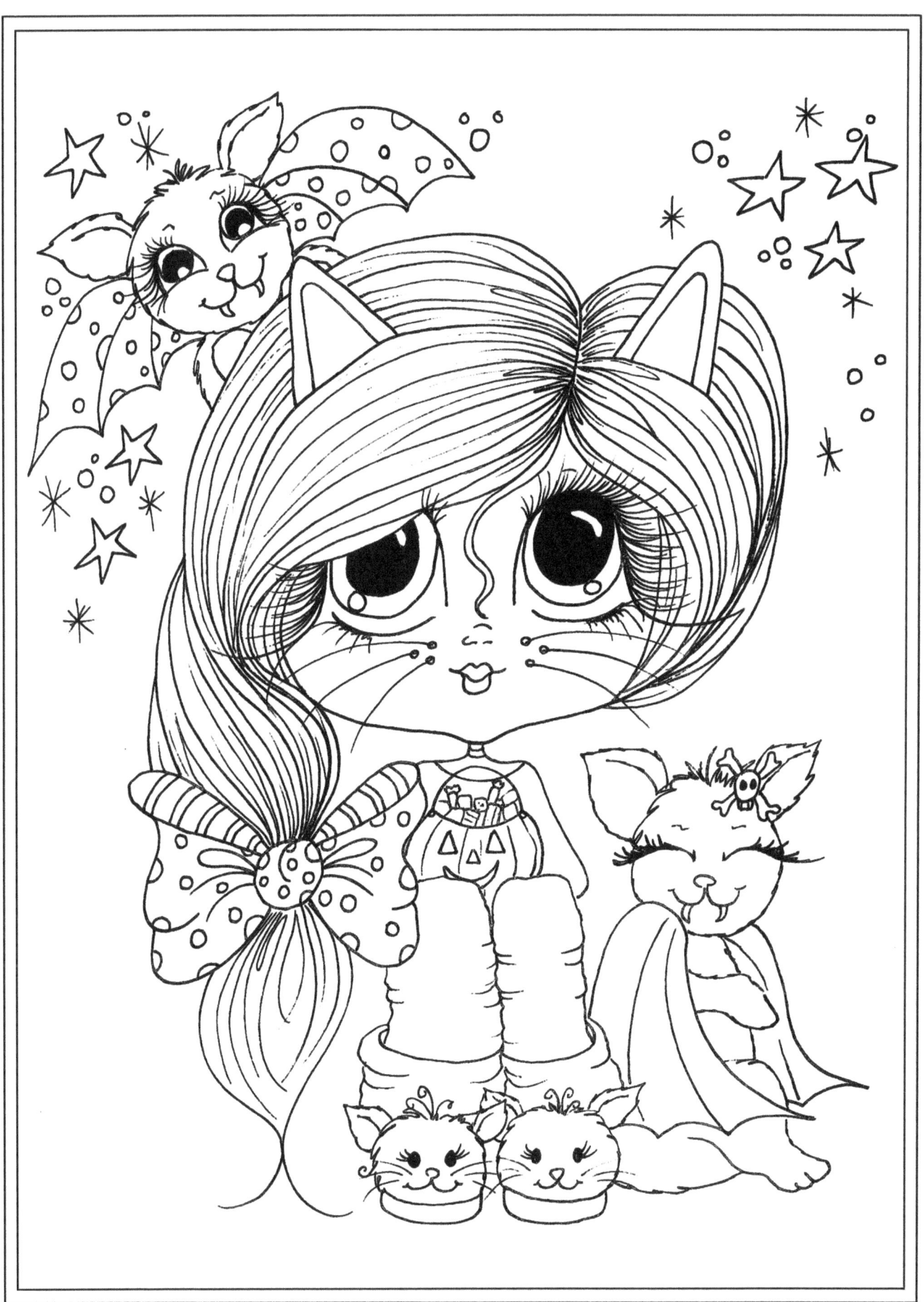

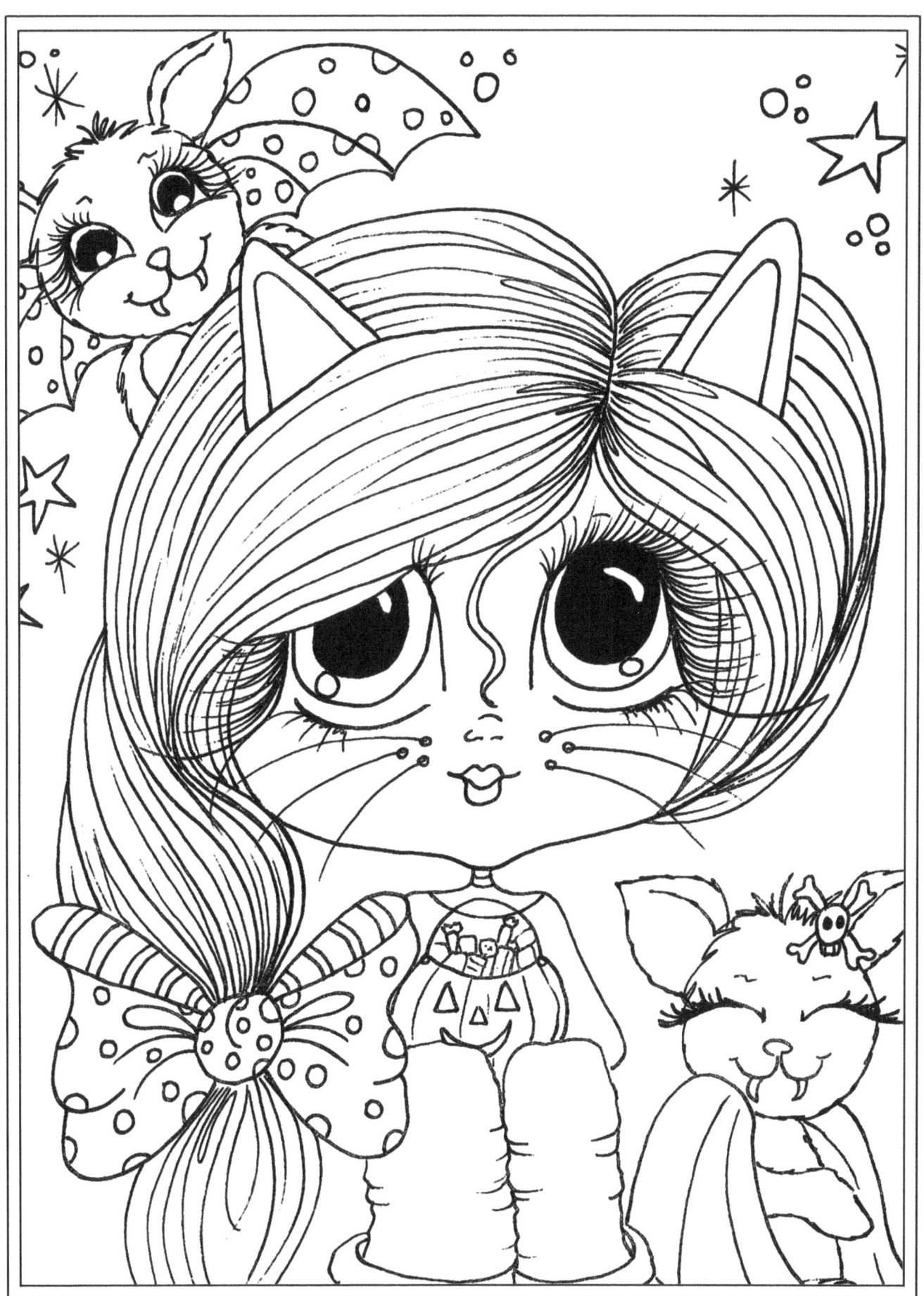

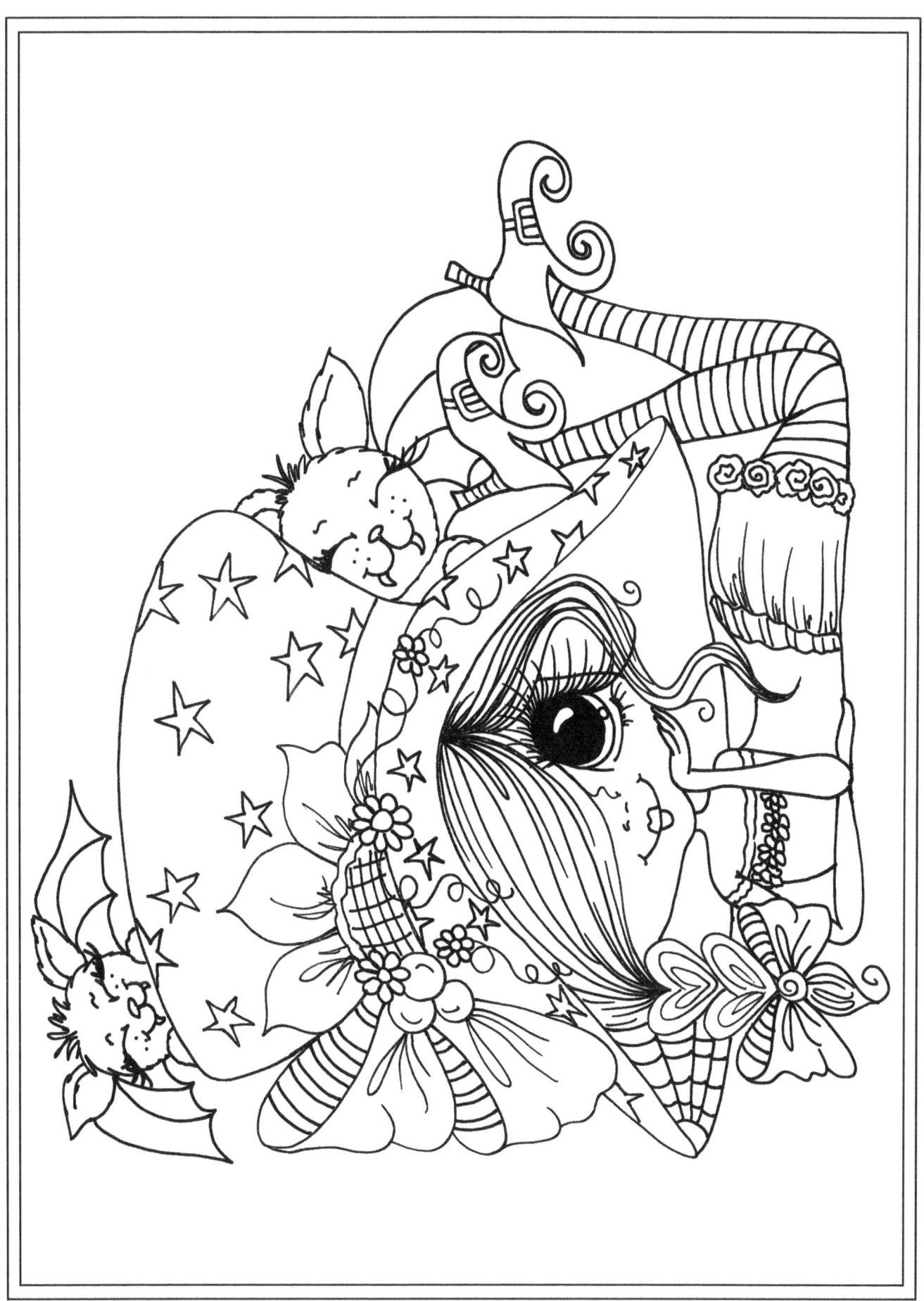

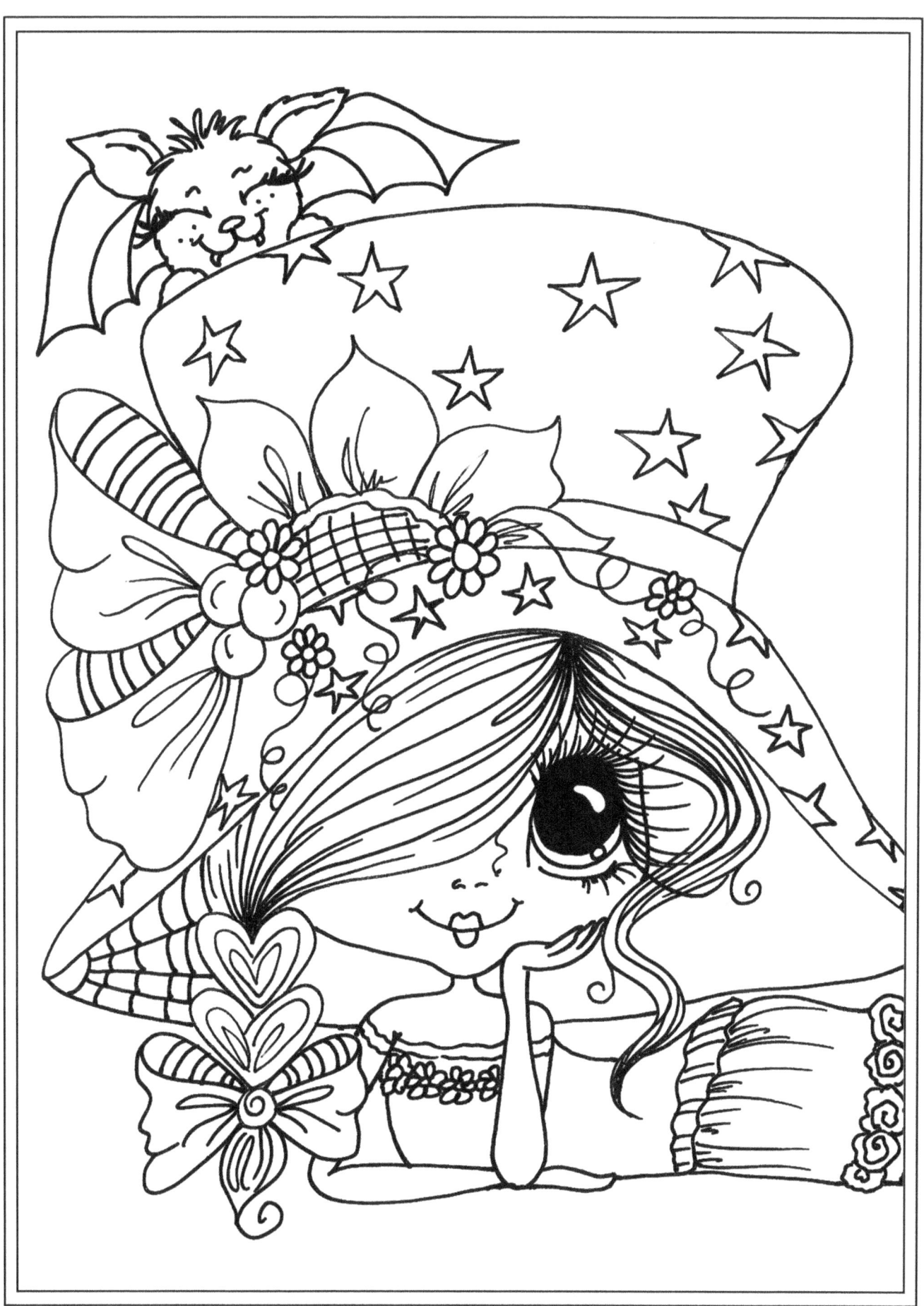

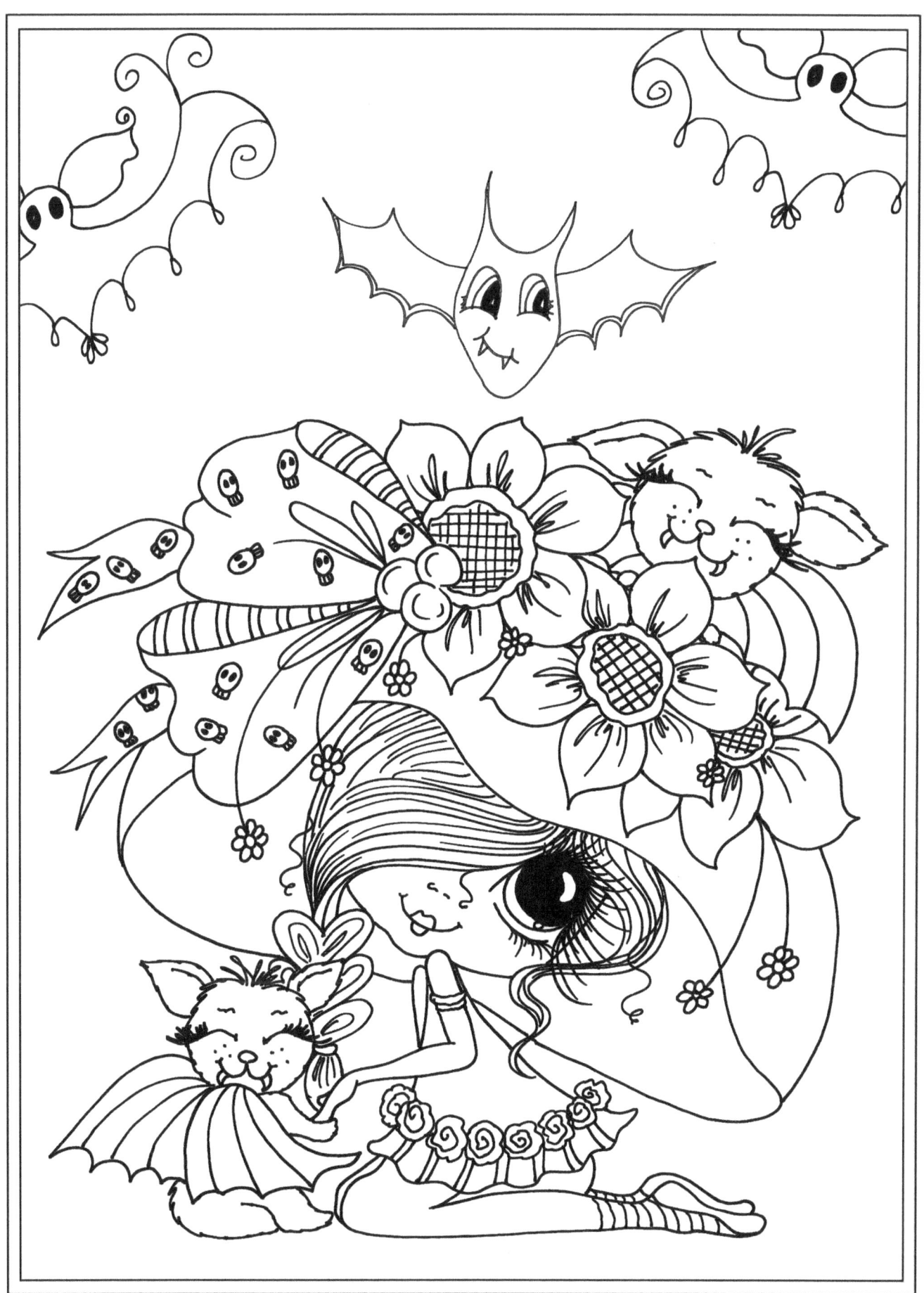

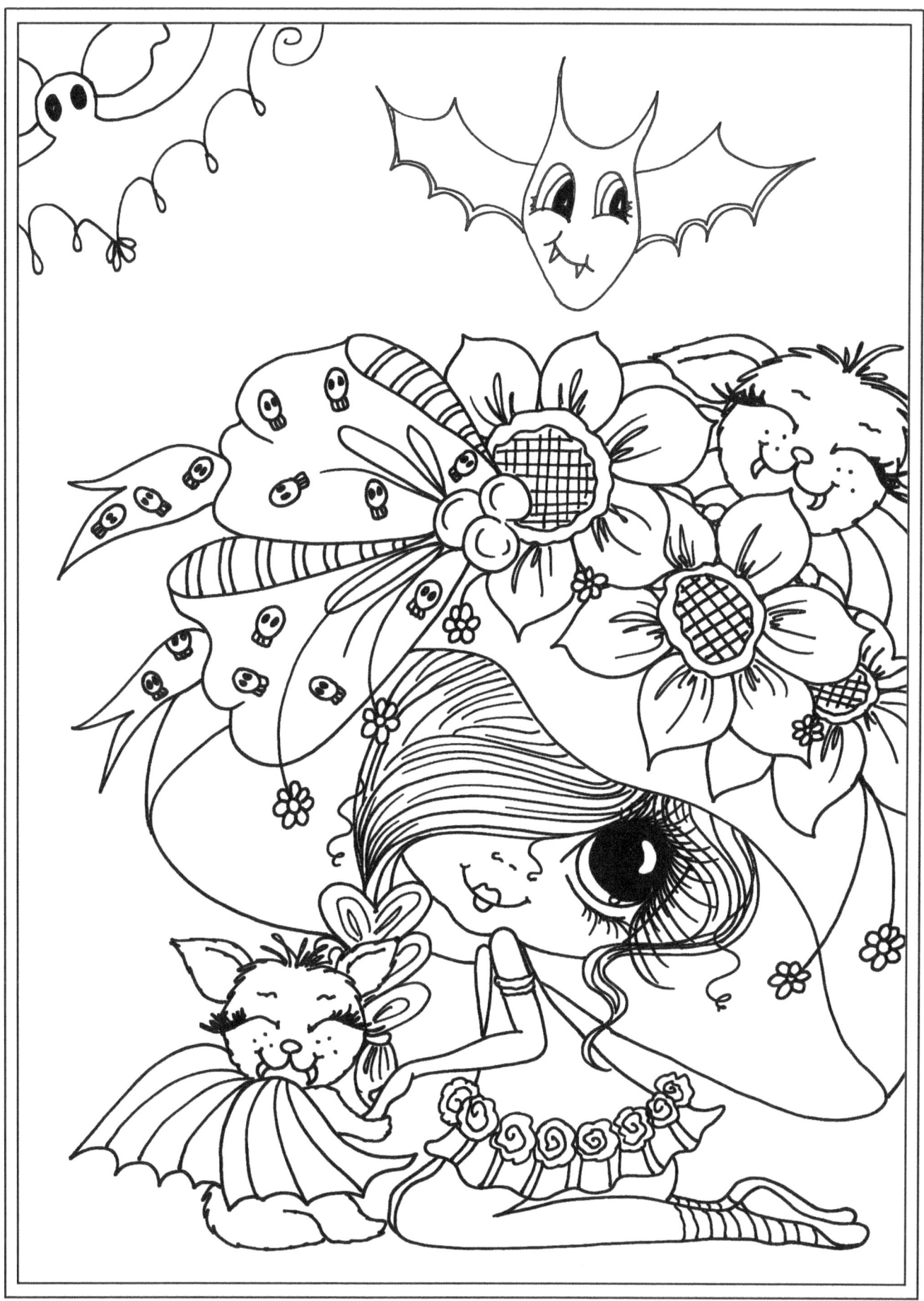

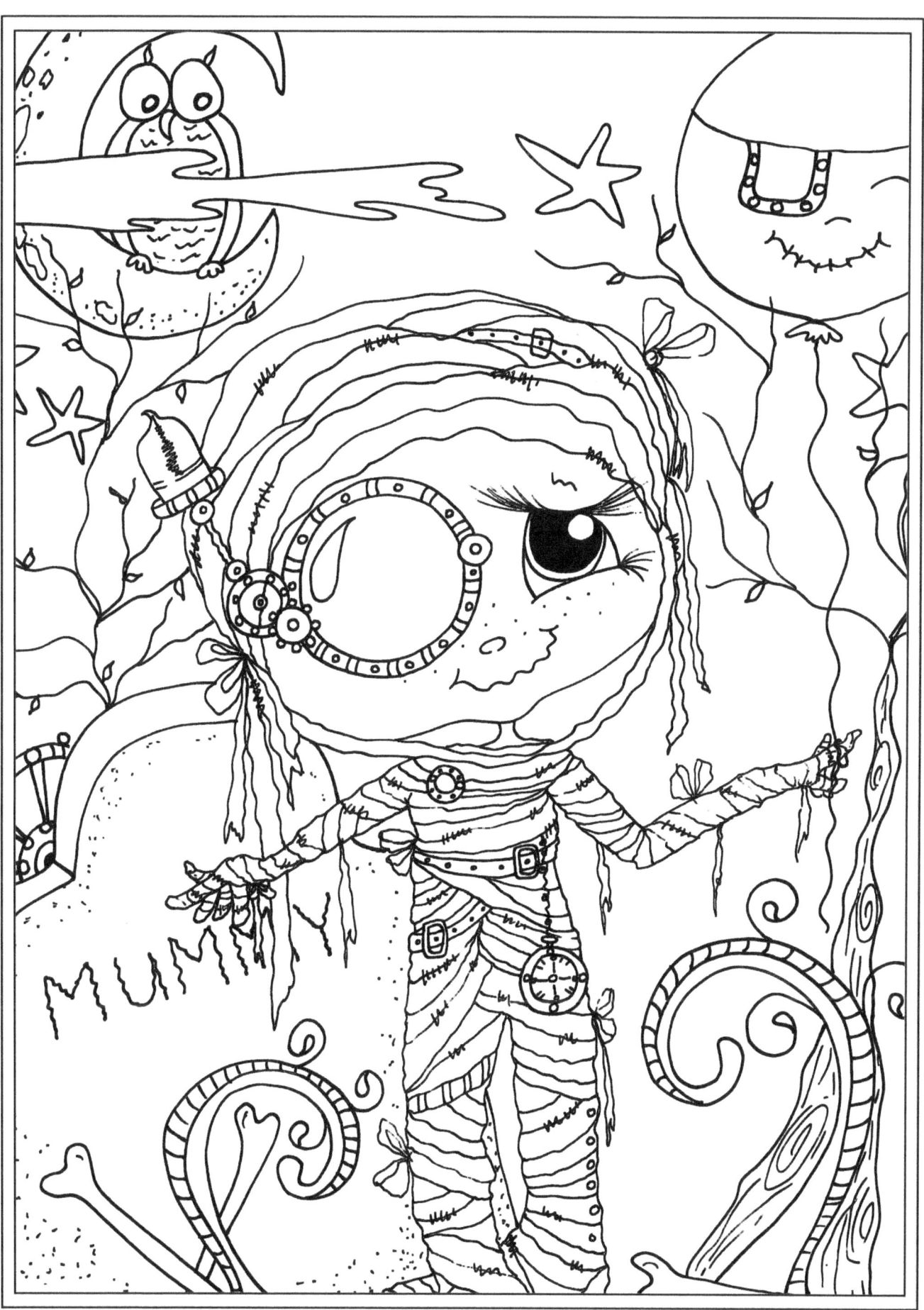

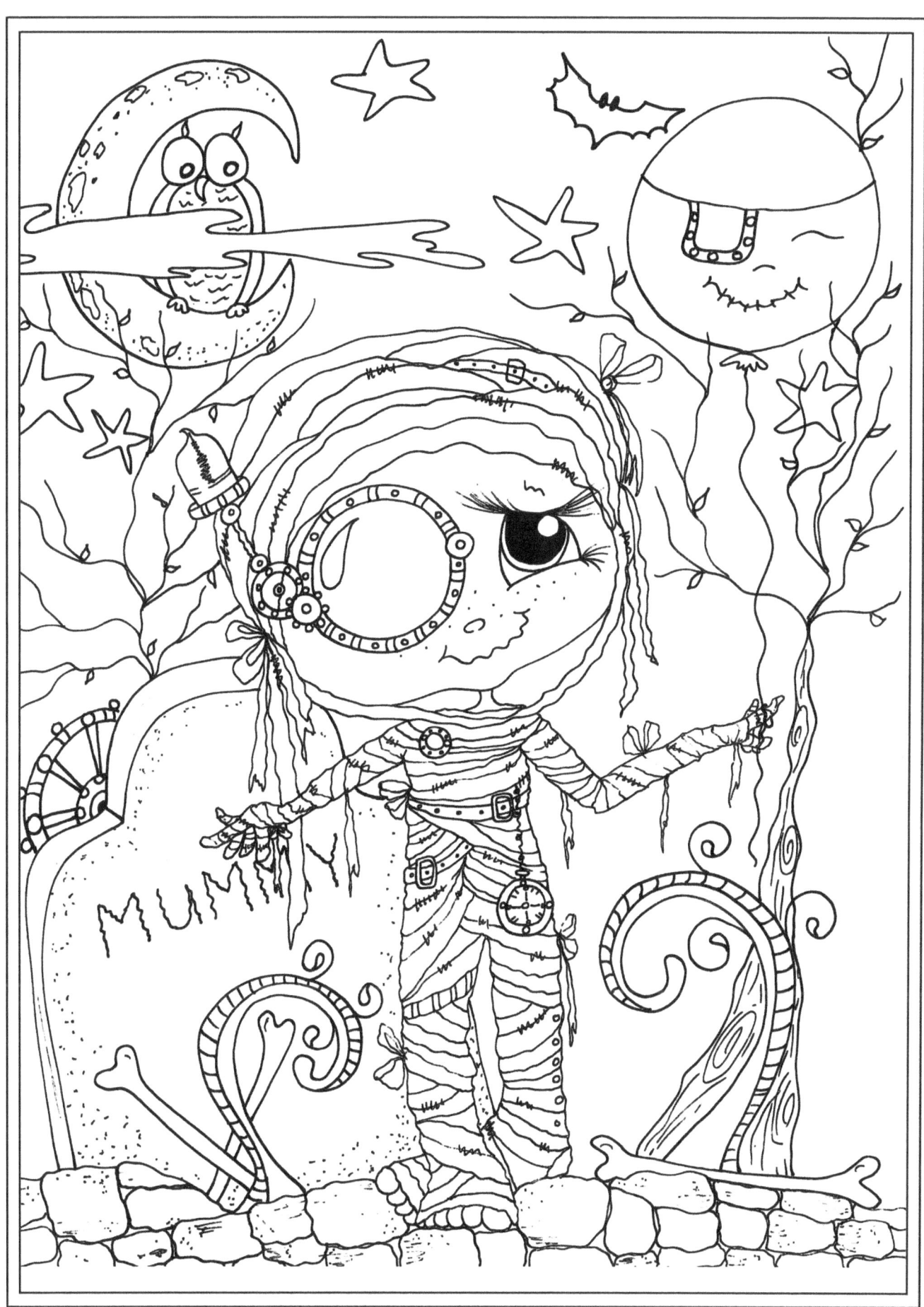

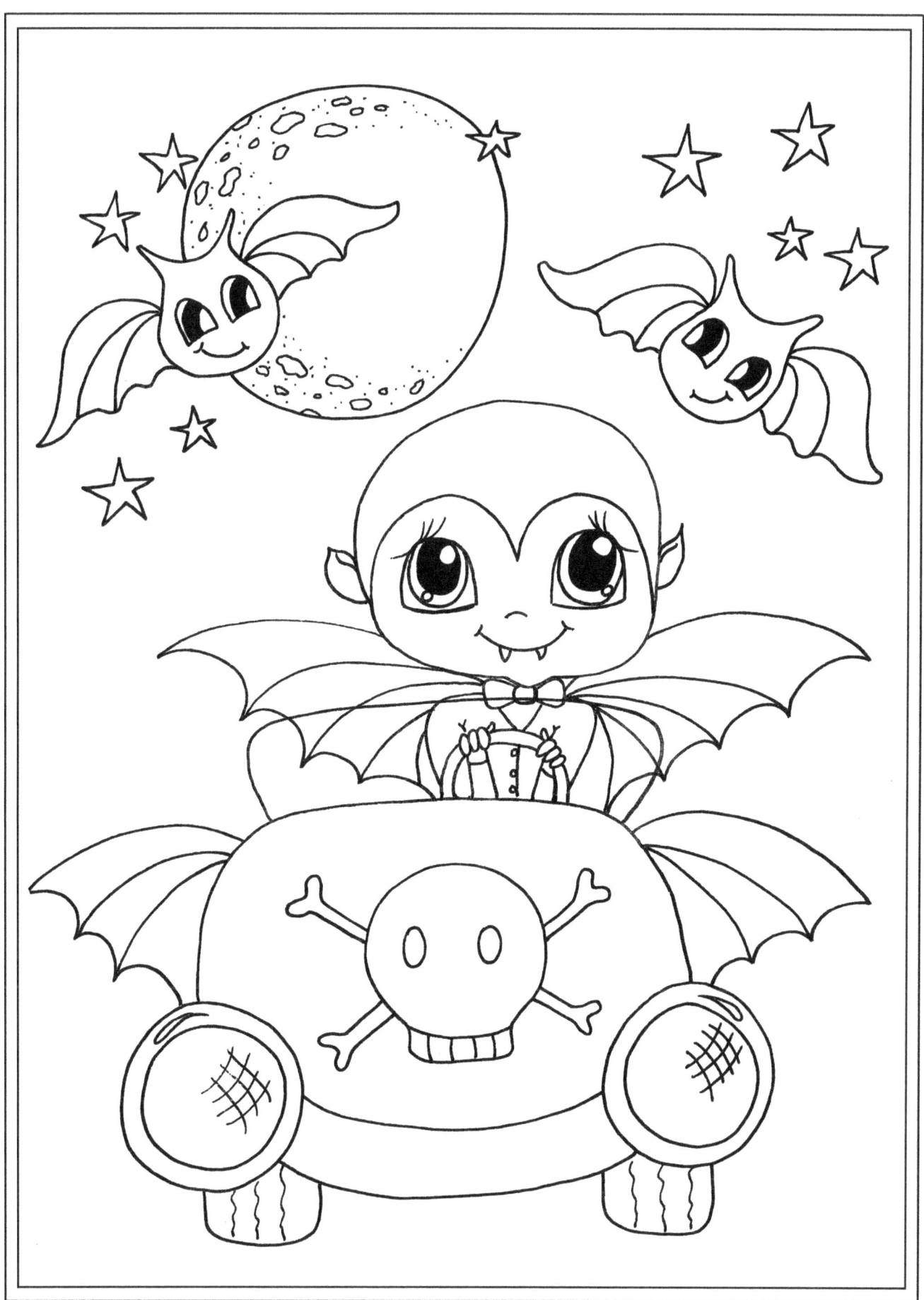

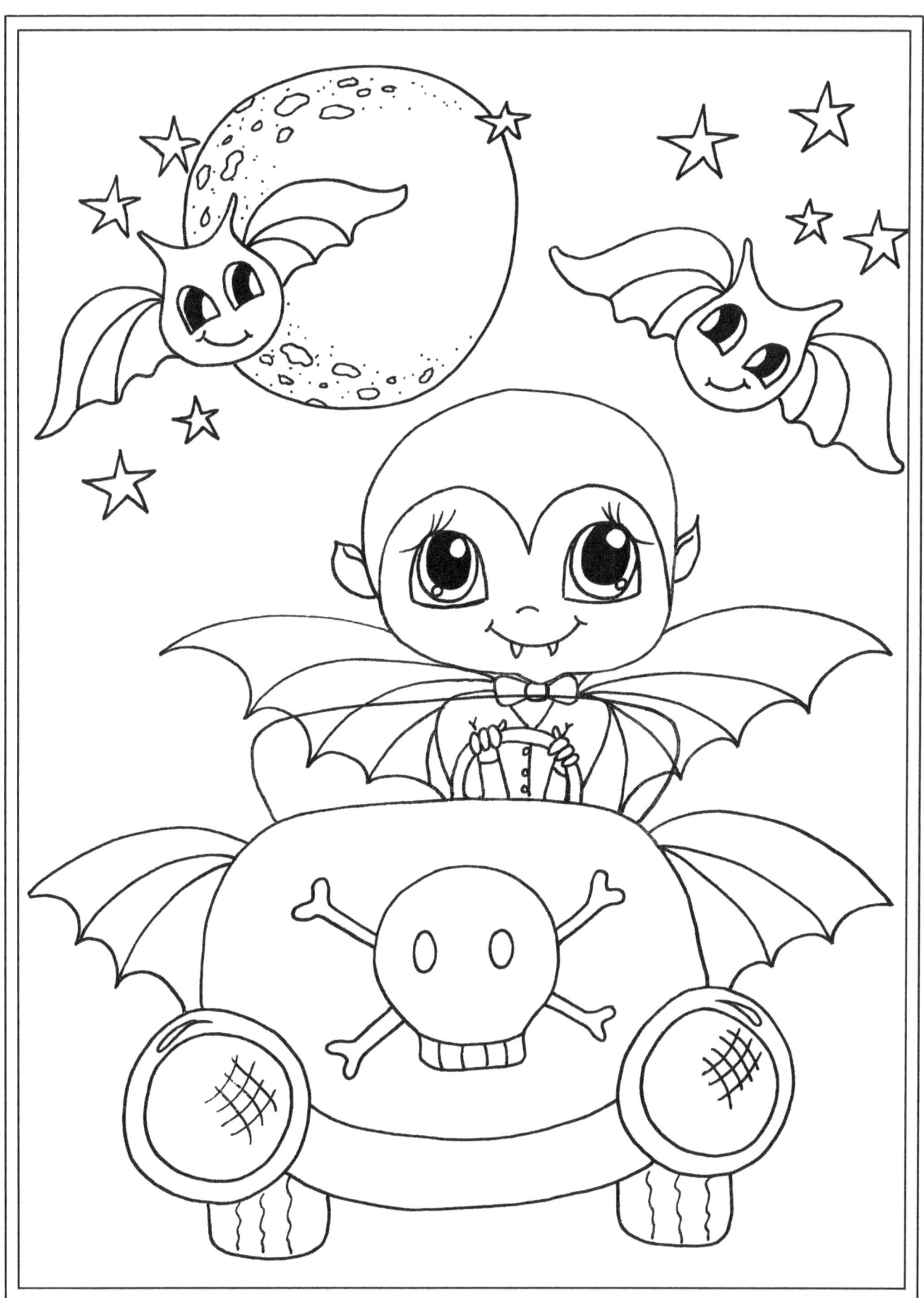

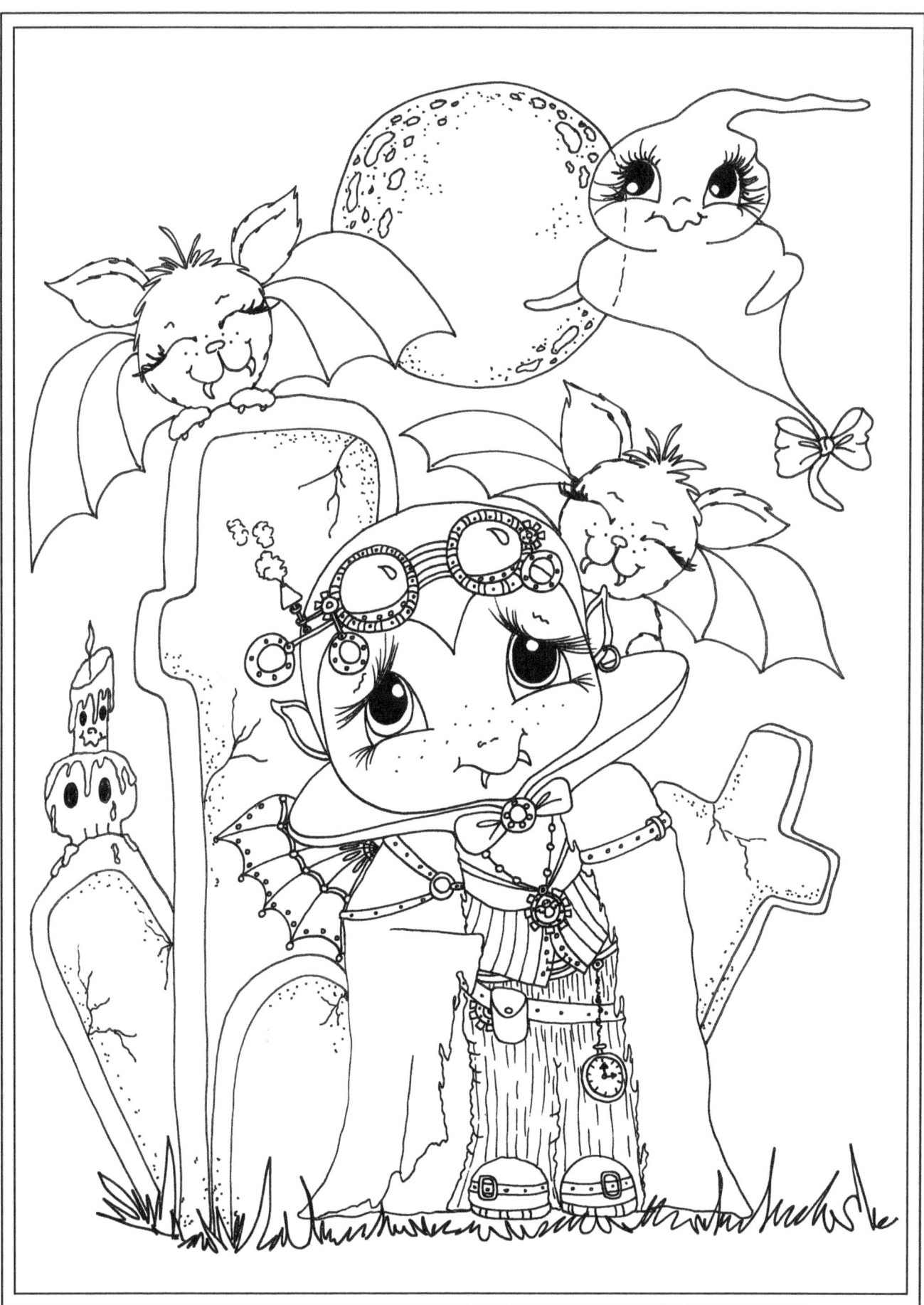

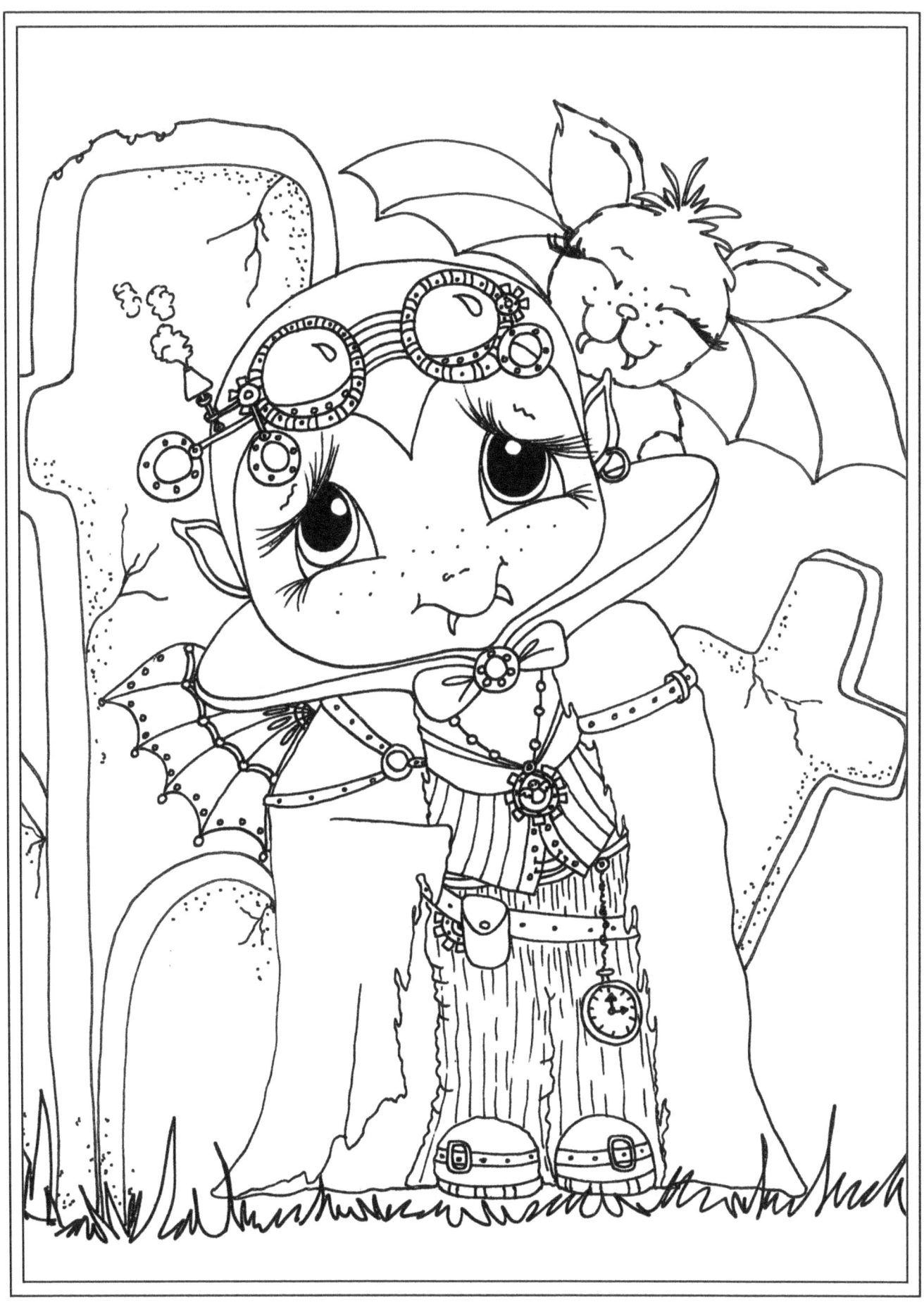

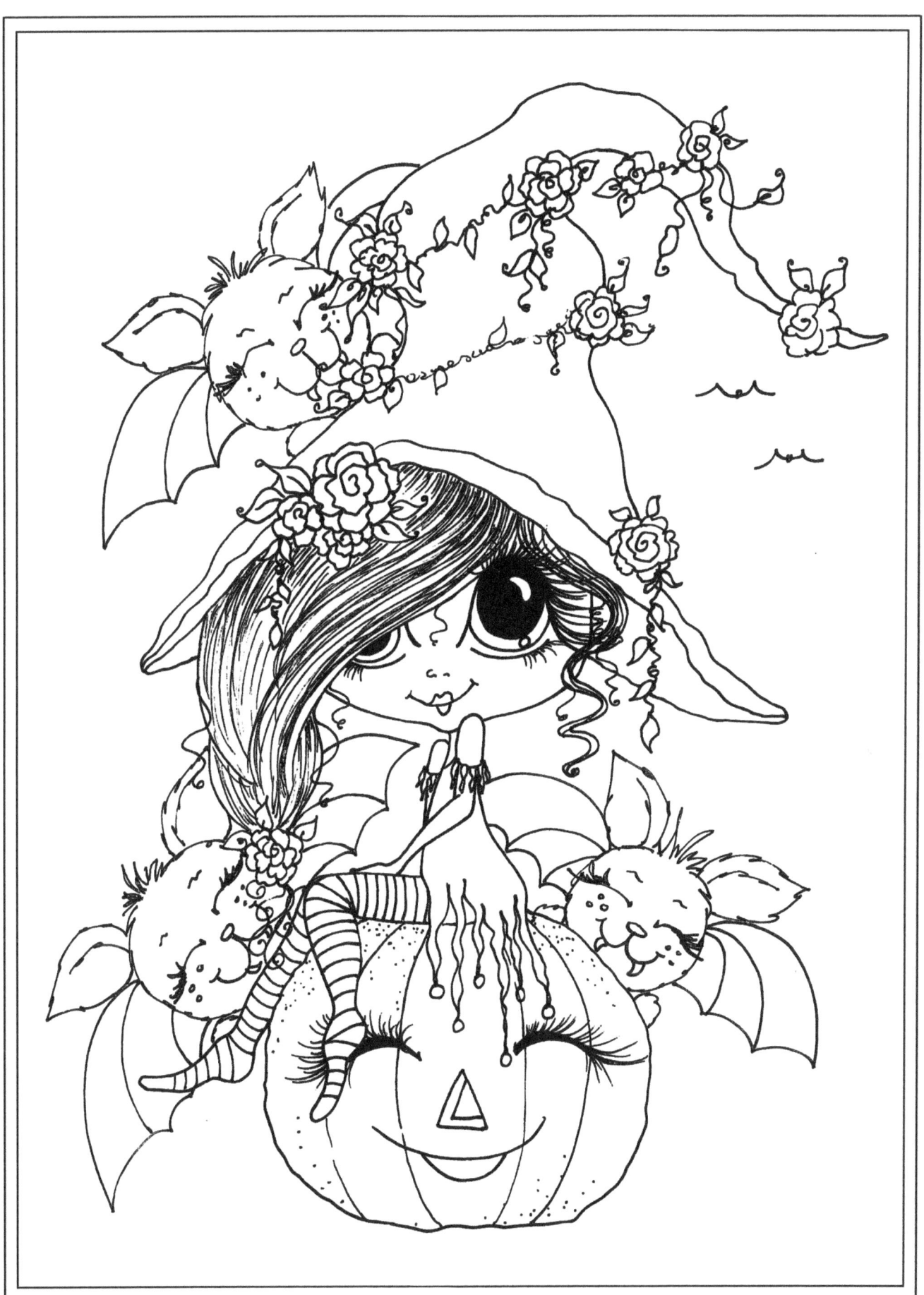

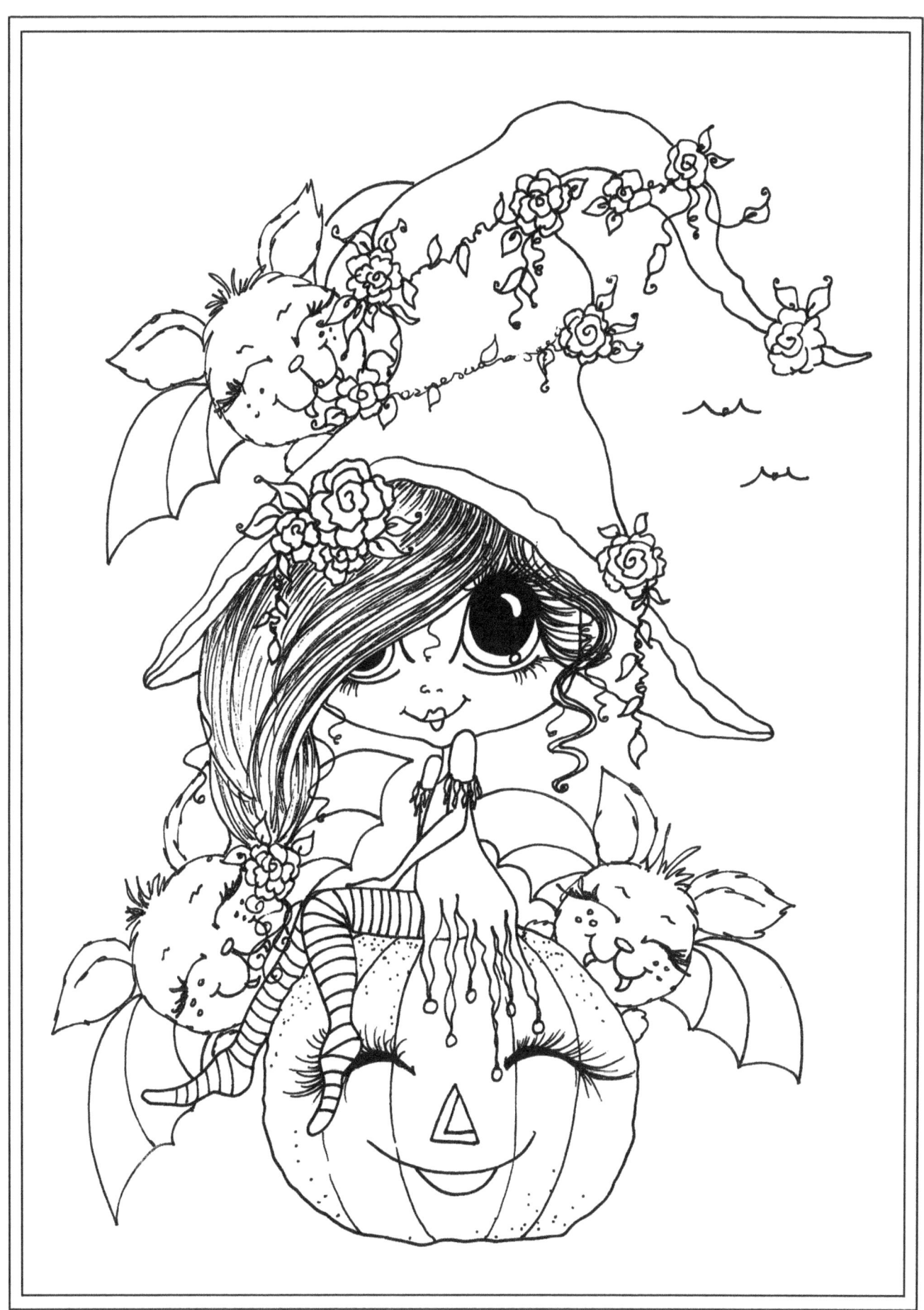

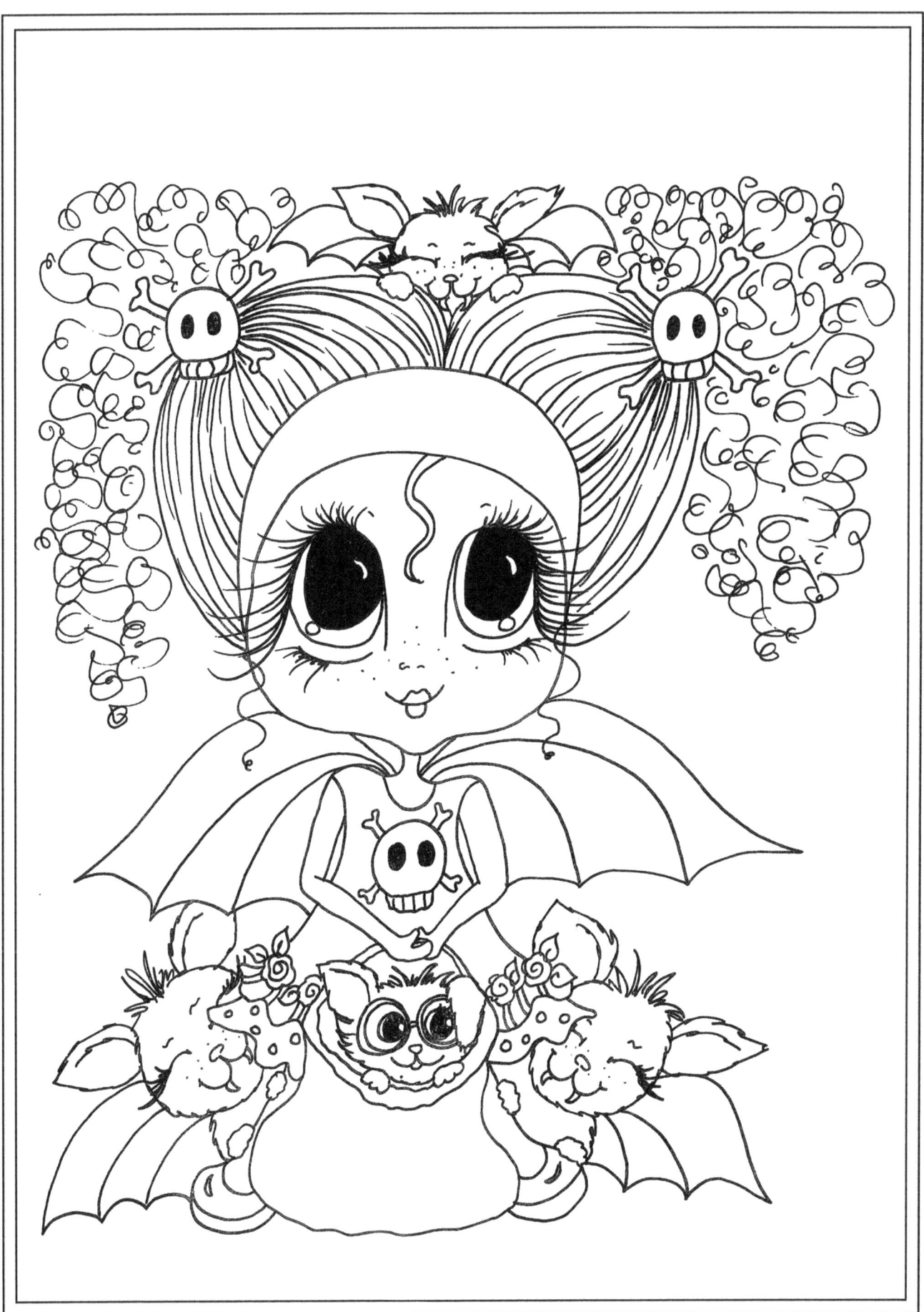

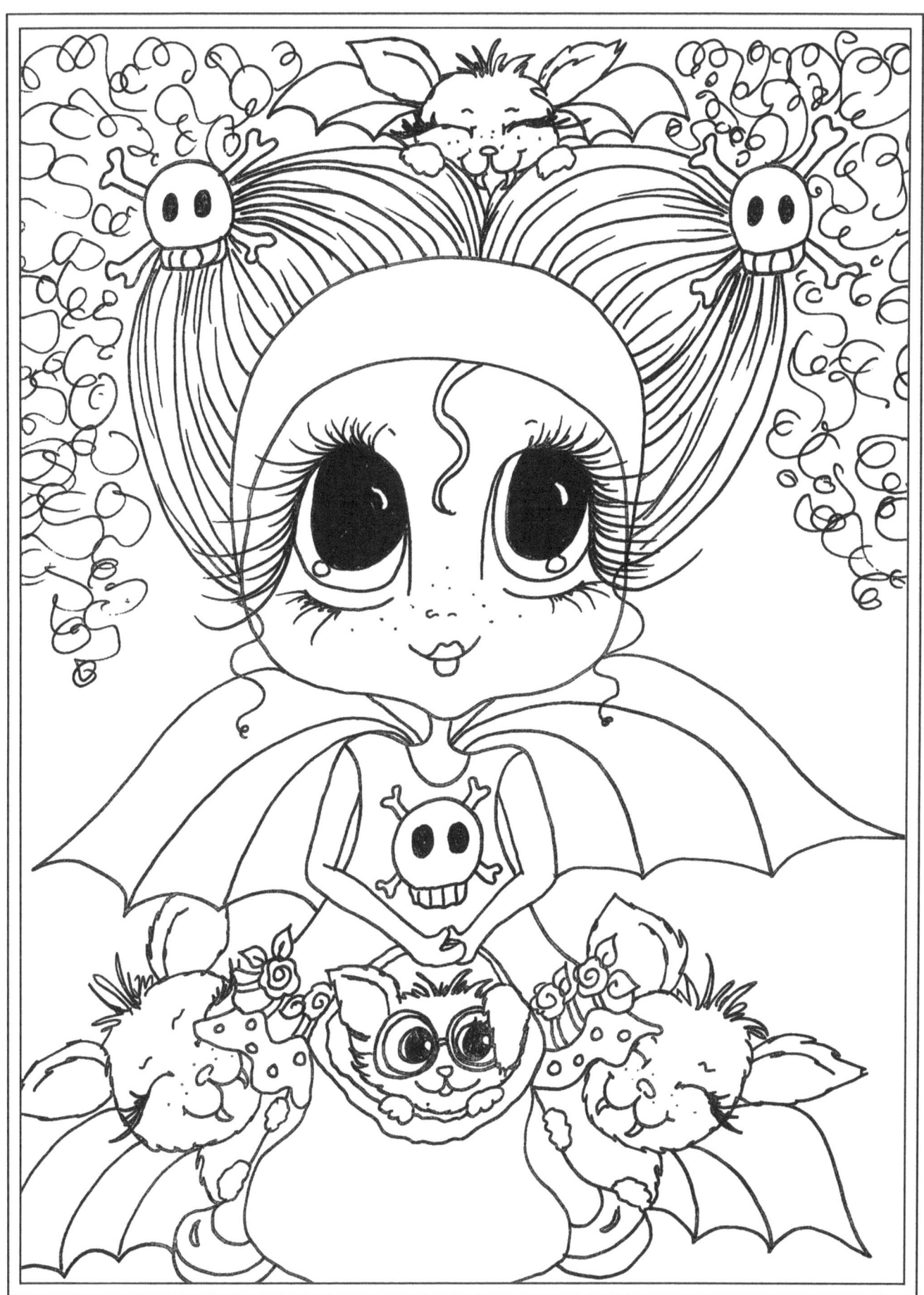